MANUAL FOR CLINICAL PSYCHOLOGY PRACTICUMS

MANUAL FOR CLINICAL PSYCHOLOGY PRACTICUMS

James Choca, Ph.D.

Chief of Psychology, Veterans Administration
Lakeside Hospital at Northwestern University Medical
School, Chicago

BRUNNER/MAZEL, INC.

THIRD PRINTING

Library of Congress Cataloging in Publication Data

Choca, James, 1945-
Manual for clinical psychology practicums.

Bibliography: p.

1. Clinical psychology—Handbooks, manuals, etc.
2. Psychodiagnostics—Handbooks, manuals, etc.
3. Psychotherapy—Handbooks, manuals, etc. I. Title.
[DNLM: 1. Psychology, Clinical. WM105 C545m]
RC467.C46 616.89 80-18731
Paper edition ISBN 0-87630-240-1 Cloth edition ISBN 0-87630-258-4

Published by
BRUNNER/MAZEL, INC.
19 Union Square
New York, New York 10003

to MORT HAMMER, Ph.D.
in the hope that his clinical
competence, enthusiasm, and
serenity have left their mark
in the pages that follow.

Introduction

For the last few years, the author has worked for the Veterans Administration Lakeside Hospital at the Northwestern University Medical Center in Chicago. He has been part of the team of professionals that works with the hospitalized psychiatric patients. The members of this team have been able to coordinate themselves well so as to function in a very synchronized and smooth fashion. This team spirit has made their work very exciting as well as productive.

During much of this time, the author's job has been to train psychology graduate students so that they could become useful members of the team. The background that these students bring with them into the clinical setting is fairly unique among the mental health disciplines. Typically they have taken a number of courses that give them a substantial theoretical background. What is usually lacking is the practical know-how in handling the clinical work.

This practical know-how is a very important area of training since it is a basic requirement for team work. Professionals cannot cooperate well with one another if they do not have some sort of system that is generally adhered to by all the members of the team. It is the knowledge of this system that allows one team member to understand the job that has been done by another member and in what way s/he can add to the treatment that the patient is receiving.

Although entire books have been written about many of the areas covered by the present work, they do not cover the mental health field in a manner that is concise and practical enough to be of service. As a result, the author found himself writing lists of instructions for the students to use in performing the different functions called upon by their clinical work. With time, these lists became the chapters of the work that follows.

The purpose of this *Manual* is to provide practical and easily understandable guidelines. An outline style was chosen as a way to present the information in a clear and orderly manner. By necessity, the coverage of any particular area will be somewhat simplistic and superficial. As students progress, they should read other sources in order to acquire the deeper understanding that eventually will be necessary. To help students choose books that will further their knowledge, references will be given often at the end of each section. A full list is also included at the end of this volume. No attempt was made to review the literature in a comprehensive way. The books chosen were those that the author found especially helpful in training students.

This *Manual* will follow an eclectic, problem-oriented approach. The author firmly believes that all schools of therapy have something to contribute and that the job of present and future therapists is to determine when a particular therapeutic strategy is most helpful. The problem-oriented approach provides a good system for organizing a clinical case in an eclectic and comprehensive manner. Because the *Manual* attempts to include all points of view, readers do not have to agree with the author's support for eclecticism in order to derive some benefits from the present work.

Acknowledgments

It should be obvious that this work contains the contributions of many individuals. The system that it teaches represents the present state of the field and is the result of the work of innumerable practitioners. Most obvious are the contributions of the other members of the staff at the hospital, especially the members of the nursing staff and doctors Elie Mangoubi, Jesus Sanchez, Mort Hammer, Luke Shanley and John Gerber. Dr. Santiago Choca was very helpful in revising the section on Drug Treatment. The section on Neuropsychological Testing was reviewed by Dr. Joseph Bleiberg. Dr. Gus Crivolio gave many useful suggestions on the whole manuscript. Drs. Theodore Millon and Robert Meagher have to be thanked for the classification of personality styles, a system that is a very important part of the present work. The suggestions and encouragement of Dr. William Reid with regard to publishing the manuscript were invaluable. The author is also grateful to all the psychology students who, while getting their training, helped to clarify what the important issues were and helped to develop ways of handling them. Finally, in a more personal way, the most significant influence has been that of Monica Choca. Her support and demand for high standards have had such an impact on the author that they undoubtedly color his whole professional life.

Contents

List of Tables

MANUAL FOR CLINICAL PSYCHOLOGY PRACTICUMS

I Basics

I.A: PSYCHODYNAMICS

1. A comprehensive mental health perspective can only be achieved if professionals take into account the whole system as much as possible.
2. The system is made up of
   a) the individual,
   b) the environment, and
   c) the interaction between the two.
3. Understanding the individual involves understanding his or her
   a) abilities,
   b) motivations—conscious or unconscious goals, and
   c) personality structure—the habitual way in which the individual views the world and interacts with it.
4. The environment includes the racial, ethnical and social aspect of the individual's
   a) family,
   b) job, and
   c) community.
5. It should be obvious that all parts of the system are intimately interrelated: The individual both influences and is influenced by the environment.
6. Professionals often choose to guide their energies toward either the individual or the system. Those that emphasize the former feel that if the individual were to change his or her mode of operation, the system would follow suit. Professionals following a systemic approach often argue that changing the system makes more sense. The present manual will present both individual and systemic points of view. The author's bias is that the professional should learn as much as possible about the client and his or her environment before deciding if the emphasis should be placed on the client, the environment, or both.

I.B: PERSONALITY STYLE THEORY

1. This section addresses itself to the concept of personality structure. Although an individual's characteristics may change from one situation to another, this concept refers to some attributes that tend to remain stable with an individual and that may be seen as the "essence" of that particular person. These attributes have also been referred to as the person's life style or personality style.
2. The personality style represents a cluster of personality traits, a cluster that can be seen together as an integrated whole. This cluster usually includes
   a) Some basic assumption about the self and the world that may or may not be at the conscious level.
   b) Some feelings about the self and the world which are usually compatible with the basic assumptions.
   c) Some habitual behaviors which are usually also compatible with the basic assumptions and feelings. By far the most important behaviors from a clinical point of view are those that affect the interpersonal relationships of the individual.
3. Every personality style has some advantages as well as some disadvantages. For instance, the assumption that life is a competitive situation where others may try to exploit us may be very appropriate when buying a used car but may be less appropriate when dealing with a spouse. Or again, the trait of orderliness gives the individual an edge when organizing a term paper but may cause the same person to be seen as a bit of a stuffed shirt in social situations.
4. The more adaptive individuals are those who
   a) have a definite personality style involving assumptions, feelings and behaviors that are within the normal range, and
   b) are flexible and able to adjust to different situations.

   This flexibility involves being able to accept assumptions, have feelings and produce behaviors that differ from the particular individual's usual tendency. Thus, for example, a well-adjusted individual who tends to be submissive and dependent can play a somewhat more dominant role in order to be successful when teaching a class.
5. Personality styles can be a source of pathology if

a) assumptions, feelings or traits are exaggerated to such a degree that they are no longer within a viable range, or
b) the individual adheres to the personality style so rigidly as to be unable to adjust to situations in which the particular personality style is not functional.

Usually, the type of pathology generated by exaggerations or rigid adherence to personality traits is considered a "Character Disorder."

6. Personality styles are so unique that a classification of possible styles will—by necessity—do an injustice to the concept. When no system is attempted, however, it is very difficult for any one but the most experienced clinician to use the concept of personality styles productively.
7. The difference between Character Disorders and personality styles should be emphasized. All individuals have some assumptions about themselves and the world around which make up their personality styles. Only a few individuals have such extreme assumptions or feelings that they are unable to function. Only those individuals would fit into the category "Character Disorder." The personality style of an individual does not imply the presence of pathology.
8. Few individuals fit nicely into one of the personality styles. Most of us combine the basic styles in proportions that are fairly unique to us. Thus, it is often advisable to take an individual's two or three most prominent personality styles into consideration.

I.C: PERSONALITY STYLES

Figure 1 maps out the scheme to be followed. The descriptions that follow were adapted from Theodore Millon (unpublished work). Table 1 gives a summary of the eight styles.

1. The Schizoid Style

We know that intellectual abilities distribute themselves in a normal curve pattern within the population. It can be argued that the ability or interest to distinguish and express emotions also exists in a dis-

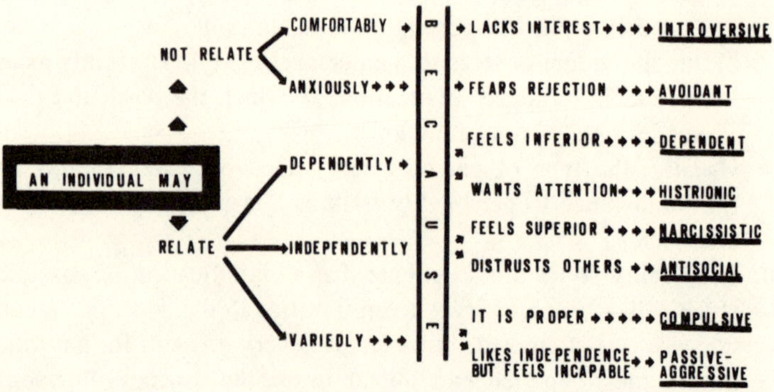

Figure 1: Basic Scheme for the Classification of Personality Styles. (Adapted from Millon, T., *Modern Psychopathology*. Philadelphia: Saunders, 1969).

proportionate fashion, with some individuals having little ability or interest in this area. Schizoid individuals are characterized by a relatively unemotional existence. When things turn out well, they don't seem particularly happy but are not too saddened by misfortune. They tend to be quiet, staying often by themselves and taking the role of passive observers. They remain uninvolved, very seldom taking sides or any strong positions. Rarely the center of attention, these individuals often fade into the social background. They have a very small number of friends and their relationships are without deep commitments. They do not fear or actively avoid people, but they are somewhat indifferent and apparently have little need to communicate or to obtain support from others. These individuals are unlikely to be passionate or lose control of their behavior, even in the most emotional situations. As a result, they may be good judges or crisis workers; they are good at any job that calls for the ability to remain detached, uninvolved and objective. Schizoid people are often viewed, however, as somewhat dull, quiet and colorless, unable to make friends and often indifferent and apathetic.

2. The Avoidant Style

Both the schizoid and the avoidant styles are similar in that they characterize people who lack interpersonal involvement in their everyday lives. In both cases, these individuals do not have close friends, tending to remain detached and isolated. In contrast to the unemotional schizoids, however, the avoidant individuals feel apprehensive when relating to others. They are usually shy and nervous in social situations. Strongly wishing to be liked and accepted by others, they fear rejection. Their concern with this rejection tends to put them on guard and make them uncomfortable, so that often social gatherings and other interpersonal situations are experienced with distaste. Relating to others is a difficult task which they often try to avoid. In so doing, however, they give up the support and affection that the avoided relationship could have brought. These individuals are sensitive, compassionate and emotionally responsive. On the other hand, they are often nervous and awkward in social situations, mistrustful of other people, lonely and isolated.

3. The Dependent Style

The life assumption of dependent individuals is that they are incapable of taking care of themselves and must find someone who is benevolent and dependable and who will support them emotionally. Individuals with this personality style have a tendency to form strong attachments to people who then take a dominant role in decision-making. They are followers rather than leaders, taking a passive role in interpersonal affairs. They shy away from highly competitive situations. Concerned with losing friends, they cover their true feelings, especially when these are aggressive or objectionable. They are unconceited individuals who try to be as congenial as possible to the people around them. Charlie Brown types, these people are usually well-liked but sometimes considered wishy-washy because of never taking a strong position on controversial issues. They can also be criticized for their tendency towards submissive dependency, for their lack of self-esteem, and for always looking outside themselves for help.

4. The Histrionic Style

Histrionics are colorful and overemotional individuals. They are people who seek stimulation, excitement and attention. They react

TABLE 1: Summary of Characteristics for the Millon Personality Styles

No.	*Style*	*Cognitive Characteristics*	*Emotional Characteristics*	*Interpersonal Characteristics*
1	Schizoid	Lack of ability and interest in communicating and understanding others in a meaningful way	Unemotional, apathetic, indifferent	Lacks friends Relates in a distant manner
2	Avoidant	Values acceptance from others to the point that rejection is seen as a terrible event	Apprehensive, uneasy, anxious	Lacks friends Relates in tentative manner and is likely to pull away
3	Dependent	Sees self as inferior, less capable or less valuable than others	Unassuming	Cooperative, submissive or dependent Tries to please others
4	Histrionic	Life becomes boring without constant stimulation	Dramatic, hyperemotional	Seeks attention Has temporary but extremely involved relationships
5	Narcissistic	Sees self as superior, more capable or more valuable than others	Proud and expansive	Assertive and dominant Seeks others that follow his or her lead

6	Antisocial	Views life as a race, to lose or to allow others to take advantage is the thing to avoid	Cold and unemotional	Self-reliant and somewhat suspicious of others Tends to use others for own benefit
7	Compulsive	Values perfection and fears making mistakes	Controlled, formal and proper	Submissive to those above Domineering and disdainful to those below
8	Passive-Aggressive	Sees self as needing others but does not think that others are more valuable or superior	Emotional fluctuations with frequent change of moods	May be cooperative but resentful or friendly and agreeable on one occasion and hostile the next

very readily to situations around them, often becoming very involved but typically the involvement does not last. This pattern of getting involved then becoming bored is repeated time after time. Histrionic people are very good at making positive first impressions. Their ability to react to unexpected situations, their alertness and interest, and their search for attention make them colorful and charming at parties or other social gatherings. Often, however, they can become too loud, exhibitionistic and overly dramatic. They can be demanding and uncontrollable, especially when they are highly involved. They may have intense emotional moments in friendships, but these friendships are often short-lived and replaced when boredom sets in. Their dependency has a very different flavor from that of the dependent individual in that they need the attention of others rather than emotional support. As a result, they may be less submissive.

5. The Narcissistic Style

The predominant assumption of narcissistic persons is that they are more competent and gifted than the rest of the people around them. This assumption gives them a flavor of mild grandiosity that colors their relationships. Usually the dominant figures in friendships, these people seek friends who support their narcissistic needs. They may relate to others in a condescending and patronizing manner. They are sociable and independent people who feel good about themselves. They are not unduly influenced by the opinions of others and are capable of making their own decisions. They are often outspoken and colorful members of society. They can be criticized, however, for being arrogant and presumptuous. They may be inconsiderate and exploitive of others, since they tend to feel that they are something special.

6. The Antisocial Style

The world view of antisocial individuals is that of a "rat race." The assumption is that everyone is after the same things (money, fame, sexual enjoyment, etc.). The only way to get one's share is to be one step ahead of the crowd. Antisocial people are self-reliant, assertive and even domineering and hostile. They are proud of this self-reliance and see themselves as "hard-headed realists." They view the world as cruel, a jungle where "might makes right." Warmth, gentleness and compassion are often seen as ineffective signs of weakness, which they avoid by being hard, cold and aggressive. Their relationships with people are often superficial and chosen for material benefits. Friendships may be terminated when their usefulness no longer exists. Because of their realistic outlook and emphasis on concrete gains, these people may be very good in business. On the positive side, they are competitive, realistic people who get things done. On the negative side, however, they are cold, domineering and insensitive people who are afraid of their own feelings of warmth and cannot trust people.

7. The Compulsive Style

The life-style of compulsive individuals is based on the premise that it would be terrible to make a mistake. Compulsive individuals are orderly and plan for the future. They are conscientious, usually well-prepared, and they get the work done on schedule. They are efficient, dependable, industrious and persistent. To those in authority, they tend to relate in an overly respectful, ingratiating and dependent manner. This style of relating often changes in the relationship with a subordinate, where they become arrogant and perfectionistic, treating the subordinate with disdain. Often these individuals believe in rules and practice self-restraint, especially when it concerns their own emotions, which are always kept under control. The overcontrol of the emotions also tends to give compulsive individuals a characteristic flavor: They are often much too formal and proper and are unlikely to open up or act spontaneously in front of others. They are sometimes seen as perfectionistic, rigid, picayune, afraid of making a mistake, and indecisive before they have a chance to study all aspects of a problem.

8. The Passive-Aggressive or Explosive Style

This style derives from two assumptions about the world that do not fit together well. The first assumption these people make is that they need to depend on others because they are not able to survive without the support or the attention of others. In this way, they are similar to the dependent or histrionic types. The contrast is created by the second premise, which is that they cannot afford to depend on others. These people often feel that others are not interested enough to be dependable or that dependence on others is not socially acceptable and will make them look bad. These assumptions may result in two different substyles. *Passive-aggressive* individuals handle the conflict by appearing cooperative on the surface but boycotting the efforts of others along the way. *Explosive* individuals vacillate between feeling that they are lucky and get more than they have a right to expect and feeling that the world has mistreated or cheated them. Their behavior changes accordingly. At times these people treat others in an agreeable and friendly manner, on other occasions they are irritable, aggressive and hostile, and at still other times, they may be full of contrition and guilt. At times they are very optimistic and see the future as bright, but this changes, seemingly without reason, into the opposite view. In their work they also vacillate: An energetic and productive mood together with high goals characterizes them at times, but at other times, they lower their goals and become less productive. These people are very flexible and changeable, sensitive and responsive to their environment, but they are also seen as moody and unpredictable.

9. Since it is often difficult to conceptualize the different personality styles, the following references are offered as approximate descriptions of the styles in literature:
   a) *Ward No. 6* by Anton Chekhov (Avoidant)
   b) *Oblomov* by Ivan Goncharov (Inadequate)
   c) *Paul's Case* by Willa Cather (Histrionic)
   d) *The Eternal Husband* by Fyodor Dostoevsky and *My Last Dutchess,* a poem by Robert Browning (Narcissistic)
   e) *Defender of the Faith* by Philip Roth (Antisocial)
   f) *The Man in a Case* by Anton Chekhov (Compulsive)
   g) *Tobias Mindernickel* by Thomas Mann (Explosive)

   The reader can also find more extensive descriptions as well as clinical vignettes in the work of Theodore Millon: *Modern Psychopathology*. Philadelphia: Saunders, 1969, and Millon, T. and Millon, R. *Abnormal Behavior and Personality*. Philadelphia: Saunders, 1974.

II Diagnostics

II.A: INTRODUCTION TO PSYCHOPATHOLOGY

1. As the individual's abilities, motivation and personality style interact with the environment, a certain amount of friction or emotional stress may develop.
2. The amount of friction that is comfortable or tolerated differs from one person to another. Also, situations that are troublesome or raise the stress felt by one individual may not be problematic at all for another.
3. As long as the amount of friction is kept below the tolerated threshold, no pathology will emerge. When this is not the case and the individual is not able to reduce the stress, psychopathology may result, as shown in Figure 2.

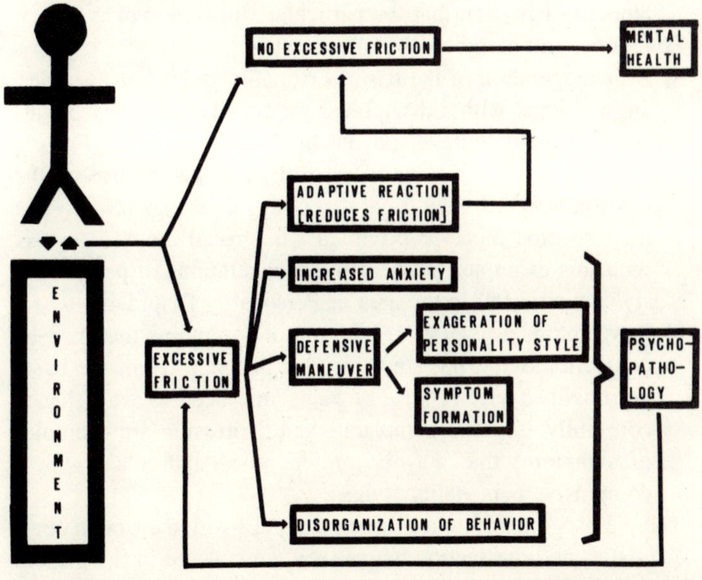

Figure 2: Flow Chart Showing the Possible Effects of the Individual's Interaction with the Environment

4. It should be noted that, as the diagram shows, pathological behavior often increases the amount of friction that the individual has with the environment. Psychopathology is often seen as having a dual role—it can be both the cause and the effect of excessive friction with the environment.
5. If we define psychopathology as consisting of the type of behavior that increases the amount of friction between the individual and the environment, we can discriminate between three different types:
   a) *Organic Pathology*—where there is something biologically wrong with the way individuals function so that they do not have the ability to behave in ways that would lower the amount of friction between themselves and the environment.
   b) *Functional Pathology*—where individuals, for psychological reasons, choose to behave in ways that do not reduce the amount of friction with the environment.
   c) *Situational Pathology*—where there is something so stressful about the situation in which individuals find themselves that there is little or nothing that they can do in order to lower the amount of friction that the particular situation evokes.
6. Functional pathology can be of two types:
   a) An exaggeration of the basic personality style. For example, an individual with a disciplined personality style may be uncomfortable with developments at his place of work. Feeling threatened, he makes an effort to tighten his control on the environment. He may insist that others do things his way, he may become more preoccupied with trivial details, etc. As with this example, most simple exaggerations of personality styles would fall in the area of Personality Disorders.
   b) A symptom formation or addition of symptoms that may be compatible with, but are somewhat different from, the basic personality style. A state of panic, the need to wash hands constantly, somatic complaints and depression are examples of symptoms that may be present in an individual with a compulsive personality style.
7. Table 2 lists the different diagnostic groups with their main characteristics and the section where they are covered in the present work.

TABLE 2: Diagnostic Groups with Their Basic Etiology, Characteristics and Place of Coverage

Main Problem Area	*Diagnostic Group*	*Main Characteristic*	*Coverage In*
Brain Functioning	Organic Mental Disorders	Biological malfunctioning	Section II. B
Psychological Functioning	Personality Disorders	Exaggeration of basic personality style	Section II. C
	Clinical Syndromes in Adults	Development of symptoms that are generally added to the basic personality	Section II. D
Environmental Stress	Reactive Disorders	Symptom addition brought about by traumatic situation	Section II. E
Mixed	Clinical Syndromes in Childhood and Adolescence	Disorders that arise in childhood or adolescence	Section II. F

8. The classification of psychopathology by the American Psychiatric Association presented in the third edition of the *Diagnostic and Statistical Manual of Mental Disorders (DSM-III)* requires the coding of data into five axes as follows:
   Axis I—Clinical Syndromes (see Section II.D).
   Axis II—Personality Disorder (see Section II.C) if present, otherwise Personality Style (see Sections I.B and I.C).
   Axis III—Physical Disorder if present
   Axis IV—Severity of Psychosocial Stressors
   Axis V—Highest Level of Adaptive Functioning during the Past Year
9. For further information on the material presented in this section, the reader is referred to:
   American Psychiatric Association. *Diagnostic and Statistical Manual*, third edition. Washington: American Psychiatric Association, 1980.
   Freedman, A. M., Kaplan, H. I., and Sadock, B. J. (Eds.) *Comprehensive Textbook of Psychiatry*. Baltimore: Williams and Wilkins, 1975.
   Coleman, J. C. *Abnormal Psychology and Modern Life*. Glenview, IL: Scott-Foresman, 1972.

II.B: ORGANIC MENTAL DISORDERS

1. Using a computer model, an organic mental disorder represents a malfunctioning of the machinery itself. In these cases, individuals do not function properly because their ability to perceive, understand or act upon a particular situation is neurologically impaired.
2. The syndromes that make up the Organic Mental Disorders (or Organic Brain Syndromes) can be grouped into seven different types as shown in Table 3. Descriptions of the individual syndromes follow below.
3. Often there are difficult diagnostic issues involved with the organic brain syndromes. First, the presence of the disorder has to be established. For this task, the Mental Status Evaluation (see Section III.B) can be used as a rough screening device. Any

TABLE 3: GROUPS OF ORGANIC BRAIN SYNDROMES

No.	*Name*	*Main Characteristic*
1	Dementias	Intellectual impairment
2	Deliriums	Disturbance of attention and thought control
3	Amnesic Syndromes	Memory impairment
4	Organic Delusional Syndromes	Presence of delusions
5	Organic Hallucinosis	Presence of hallucinations
6	Organic Emotional Syndromes	Disturbance of emotional functioning
7	Intoxications	Disturbance of intellectual and motor functioning due to substance use
8	Withdrawals	Disturbance of intellectual and motor functioning due to withdrawal of substance from the system

NOTE: If a disturbance occurs that does not fit into any of the above groups but for which there is evidence of organic etiology, it would be diagnosed as "Other Organic Brain Syndrome" (294.80).

questionable findings should be further documented with neuropsychological testing (see Section III.E). Finally, a neurological exam should be obtained through consultation with a neurologist.

4. After the presence of an organic syndrome has been established, it is often necessary to rule out the existence of another disorder. This task is often hard because many neurological impairments present clinical pictures that resemble emotional syndromes. A good clinical history and evaluation are the tools used to accomplish this task. If the clinical picture coincides with any of the functional disorders, it is necessary to document that the behaviors in question were present before the onset of the organicity. If this is not the case, it is assumed that the personality change was the direct or indirect result of organicity.
5. The Mental Retardations are usually the result of neurological

impairments. However, under the present system, they are considered Disorders of Childhood and Adolescence instead of Organic Brain Syndromes.

6. The Organic Brain Syndromes may be temporary or permanent, depending on their etiology. Further information regarding specific neurological disorders can be obtained by consulting:
   Freedman, A. M., Kaplan, H. I., and Sadock, B. J. (Eds.) *Comprehensive Textbook of Psychiatry*. Baltimore: Williams and Wilkins, 1975.
7. A good book for a general background on neurology is:
   Gardner, E. *Fundamentals of Neurology, A Psychophysiological Approach*. Philadelphia: Saunders Co., 1975.
8. In the descriptions that follow, the italicized terms are the official diagnoses used.

Descriptions

1. Dementias:

A *Dementia* is a severe deterioration of memory, judgment and abstract thinking ability that is due to an organic condition. When appropriate, one of the specific disorders that follow should be used:

a) *Primary Degenerative Dementia*—a progressive dementia of an unknown cause.
b) *Multi-Infarct Dementia*—involves the deterioration of some intellectual functions but not of others and is accompanied by focal neurological signs.
c) *Alcohol or Substance Abuse Dementia*—occurs in an individual who has taken alcohol or another substance for a prolonged period of time even after the individual is well detoxified.

2. Deliriums:

A *Delirium* is a fluctuating disturbance of attention, memory and orientation which develops rapidly and is the result of an organic condition. It is usually accompanied by a sleep disorder, changes in psychomotor activity or perceptual misinterpretations. When the delirium is related to a substance abuse, one of the disorders that follow should be used:

a) *Alcohol Withdrawal Delirium (Delirium Tremens)*—takes place in an individual who stops alcohol ingestion after a period of heavy drinking. It is usually accompanied by tachycardia, sweating and elevated blood pressure.
b) *Barbiturate Withdrawal Delirium*—the same as the Alcohol Withdrawal Delirium, but the drug used was a barbiturate.
c) *Amphetamine or Other Substance Delirium*—follows intake of a toxic substance.

3. Organic Amnesic Syndromes:

An *Organic Amnesic Syndrome* is a disturbance of the recent memory function where attention, judgment and abstract thinking remain unimpaired, as long as it is thought to be the result of an organic condition. When the syndrome is connected to substance abuse, one of the disorders that follow should be used:
a) *Alcohol Idiosyncratic Intoxication*—involves the inability to recall events that took place after the individual had ingested a small amount of alcohol.
b) *Alcohol, Barbiturate or Other Substance Amnesic Syndrome*—Organic Amnesic Syndrome that develops after prolonged use of toxic substance.

4. Organic Delusional Syndromes:

A *Delusional Organic Syndrome*—involves false beliefs and results from an organic condition. A Delusional Syndrome may be an *Amphetamine, Hallucinogen, Cannabis or Other Substance Delusional Syndrome* if it develops as a result of recent drug intake.

5. Organic Hallucinatory Syndrome:

An *Organic Hallucinatory Syndrome*—involves a false perception, while the individual is alert and does not show any other intellectual deficits, and is thought to be the result of an organic condition. It may be an *Alcohol, Hallucinogen or Other Substance Hallucinatory Syndrome* if it develops as a result of recent drug intake.

6. Organic Emotional Syndromes:

An *Organic Emotional Syndrome* involves the appearance of a manic

or depressive state (see Section II.D) that is thought to be caused by an organic condition. When appropriate, the diagnosis of Hallucinogen or Other Substance Abuse Emotional Syndrome should be used:
Organic Personality Syndrome is a disorder involving fluctuations of mood, impulsiveness, apathy or suspiciousness that are due to organic damage.

7. *Intoxications:*

Intoxications are behavioral disorders, usually accompanied by some physical symptoms as well, that result from the intake of specific drugs. They are classified according to the drug used as follows:
a) *Alcohol Intoxication*
b) *Barbiturate Intoxication*
c) *Opioid Intoxication*
d) *Cannabis (Marijuana) Intoxication*
e) *Cocaine Intoxication*
f) *Amphetamine Intoxication*
g) *Caffeine Intoxication*
h) *Other Substance Intoxication*

8. *Drug Withdrawal:*

Some drugs cause a physical dependence so that, when an individual takes the drug for a period of time and then stops taking the drug, a number of physical symptoms may result. Withdrawals are classified according to the drug that is being withdrawn as follows:
a) *Alcohol Withdrawal* (This diagnosis is only used when delirium is not present (see #2 above)
b) *Barbiturate Withdrawal*
c) *Opioid Withdrawal*
d) *Amphetamine Withdrawal*
e) *Tobacco Withdrawal*
f) *Other Substance Withdrawal*

II.C: PERSONALITY DISORDERS

1. The Personality Disorders or Character Disorders are mainly exaggerations of the basic personality style. In fact, many of the

syndromes differ from the Millon Personality Styles presented in Section I.C only as far as the magnitude of the personality traits.

2. The Paranoid, Schizotypal and Borderline Personality Disorders do not have a personality style equivalent. Nevertheless, they are often exaggerations of the personality style of the individual. For instance, the Paranoid Personality Disorder is often an exaggeration of an antisocial trait or of ambivalent, passive-aggressive feelings.
3. There are three disorders in childhood and adolescence that are rough equivalents of Personality Disorders (Introverted Disorder of Childhood, Shyness Disorder and the Conduct Disorders). These, however, will be covered in Section II.F under Clinical Syndromes in Children and Adolescents.

Descriptions

1. *Schizoid Personality Disorder*: Disorder characterized by a long history of withdrawal and isolation with few, if any, close friendships. These individuals lack the capacity and interest in relating to others and appear apathetic and unemotional.
2. *Avoidant Personality Disorder*: Disorder characterized by a fear of and hypersensitivity to rejection by others, with a resulting reluctance to establish close friendships. The pattern has to be fairly permanent and is usually accompanied by low self-esteem and a desire to be liked and accepted.
3. *Dependent Personality Disorder*: Disorder characterized by a long-term pattern of submissive and dependent behaviors in an individual who lacks self-confidence and who is uncomfortable when alone or unsupported.
4. *Histrionic Personality Disorder*: Disorder characterized by a long-term pattern of dramatic, overly emotional behaviors together with interpersonal difficulties, as exemplified by superficiality, demandingness, egocentrism or dependency and helplessness.
5. *Narcissistic Personality Disorder*: Disorder characterized by a long-term pattern of grandiose and exhibitionistic behaviors, inability to accept criticism and a tendency to expect that others will be submissive and attentive.

6. *Antisocial Personality Disorder*: Disorder characterized by a long-term pattern of antisocial behaviors such as criminal activities, rebelliousness, substance abuse, irresponsibility, exploitiveness in interpersonal relations and instability of location and occupation in an individual who is not mentally retarded, schizophrenic or paranoid.
7. *Compulsive Personality Disorder*: Disorder characterized by a long-term history of preoccupation with trivial details, discomfort when the person is not in control, rigidity and inability to make decisions expediently, difficulty in expressing tenderness and excessive devotion to work.
8. *Passive-Aggressive Personality Disorder*: Disorder characterized by a deeply ingrained obstructional or negativistic attitude so that the individual is superficially compliant but undoes agreements through procrastination, intentional inefficiency, etc.
9. *Schizotypal Personality Disorder*: Disorder characterized by a long-term history of eccentricity and withdrawal without psychotic symptoms. These behaviors may include superstitiousness, ideas of reference, tangentiality or circumstantiality, inappropriate emotional responses or suspiciousness.
10. *Paranoid Personality Disorder*: Disorder characterized by a long-term pattern of suspiciousness, a tendency to misconstrue normal actions as hostile, excessive sensitivity to setbacks and inclination to excessive self-importance.
11. *Borderline Personality Disorder*: Disorder characterized by a lack of a goal-directed pattern of behavior. It may include impulsivity and unpredictability, self-destructive behaviors, intense but unstable personal relationships, lack of clear self-identity, marked shifts of mood, chronic feelings of meaninglessness and discomfort when alone. These problems have to be characteristic of long-term functioning.
12. *Other Personality Disorder*: Personality Disorder that differs from or represents a mixture of the disorders described above.

II.D CLINICAL SYNDROMES IN ADULTS

1. Exaggerations of the basic personality style can, in some cases,

be part of the disorders presented in this section. For example, the Obsessive-Compulsive Anxiety Disorder may involve repeated hand-washing, which can be seen as an extreme exaggeration of the cleanliness of the compulsive personality style. Most typically, however, these syndromes represent pathology that is added on to the basic personality style.

2. In spite of the fact that most of the symptoms that are covered in this chapter are additions to the basic personality style, the individual's style remains an important aspect in understanding the behavior. For instance, a Paranoid Schizophrenic Disorder in a Compulsive individual is often colored by a rigidity, a righteousness or a perfectionism that is an obvious reminder of the basic personality style. In comparison, the same disorder in a Narcissistic individual is typically flavored by grandiosity and feelings of omnipotence.
3. Table 4 shows the basic classification scheme. Descriptions of the different disorders follow. It should be noted that all of the clinical syndromes are "functional disorders" and only to be used when the behavior in question is not the result of an organic brain syndrome or other physical abnormality.
4. In the descriptions that follow, the italicized terms are the official diagnoses used.

Descriptions

1. Substance Abuse Disorders:

The disorders that follow involve an impairment of social or occupational functioning due to a psychological dependence on and frequent use of a particular drug. The substance abuse disorders are classified according to the drug used as indicated below.

a) *Alcohol Abuse Disorder*
b) *Cannabis (Marijuana) Abuse Disorder*
c) *Hallucinogen Abuse Disorder*
d) *Barbiturate Abuse Disorder*
e) *Opioid Abuse Disorder*
f) *Cocaine Abuse Disorder*
g) *Amphetamine Abuse Disorder*
h) *Other Substance Abuse Disorder*

TABLE 4: Basic classification for the Clinical Syndromes in adults with the exception of the Personality Disorders which are covered in Section II. C. The classification is adapted from the DSM-III of the American Psychiatric Association. A group number was given to facilitate finding the individual syndromes in the pages that follow.

No.	*Disorder Group*	*Basic Characteristics*
	DRUG RELATED DISORDERS	
1	Substance Abuse Disorders	Impairment of functioning as a result of intoxication
2	Substance Dependence Disorders	Physical dependence resulting from substance abuse
	PSYCHOSES	
3	Schizophrenic Disorders	Functional disorganization of the thinking process
4	Paranoid Disorders	Persecutory delusions or delusions of jealousy without disorganization of the thinking process
5	Other Psychoses	Atypical and mixed psychotic disorders
	NEUROSES	
6	Affective Disorders	Disorders involving changes in mood
7	Anxiety Disorders	Disorders involving anxiety, panic states or irrational fears
8	Factitious Disorders	Physical or psychological complaints under voluntary control
9	Somatoform Disorders	Physical complaints without organic causes and not under voluntary control
10	Dissociative Disorders	Disorders of consciousness or identity
	SEXUAL DISORDERS	
11	Gender Identity Disorders	Psychological discomfort with the individual's anatomic sex
12	Ego-Dystonic Homosexuality	Psychological discomfort resulting from perceived homosexual tendencies
13	Paraphilias	Sexual arousal being produced by unusual sexual objects
14	Sexual Dysfunctions	Inability to function adequately in sexual relationships
	OTHER DISORDERS	
15	Impulse Control Disorders	Failure to resist harmful impulses

2. Substance Dependence Disorders:

The disorders that follow involve a physical dependency on the use of the drug as characterized by the need to increase the amount of the drug taken and by the appearance of withdrawal symptoms if the drug is discontinued. These disorders are classified by the type of drug used as follows:

a) *Alcohol Dependence*
b) *Cannabis (Marijuana) Dependence*
c) *Barbiturate Dependence*
d) *Opioid Dependence*
e) *Cocaine Dependence*
f) *Amphetamine Dependence*
g) *Other Substance Dependence*

3. Schizophrenic Disorders:

Schizophrenic disorders are characterized by a disturbance of the thought process that is severe enough to cause a significant impairment in the individuals' abilities to work, maintain social relations or take care of themselves. The disturbance of the thought process may include delusions, hallucinations, incoherence, or looseness of associations with flat or inappropriate emotional responses. Five schizophrenic disorders are presently recognized:

a) *Disorganized Schizophrenic Disorder*—further characterized by frequent incoherence and an inappropriate affect.
b) *Catatonic Schizophrenic Disorder*—further characterized by rigidity, posturing, stupor, mutism or uncontrollable excitement.
c) *Paranoid Schizophrenic Disorder*—further characterized by grandiose or persecutory delusions, delusions of jealousy or hallucinations with persecutory or grandiose content.
d) *Undifferentiated Schizophrenic Disorder*—to be used when a schizophrenic individual cannot be characterized by any of the three disorders given above.
e) *Residual Schizophrenic Disorder*—to be used with individuals who have reintegrated after presenting a clearly schizophrenic picture and who still show some residues of the previous symptomatology.

4. *Paranoid Disorders:*

a) *Paranoia*—characterized by persistent persecutory delusions or delusions of jealousy without a mood disturbance or any other disturbance of the thought process (no hallucinations, incoherence, loosening of associations, confused thinking or inappropriate emotions).
b) *Shared Paranoid Disorder*—develops as a result of a close relationship with a person who already has the delusional system.
c) *Acute Paranoid Disorder*—develops suddenly and for a limited period of time, usually as a response to a difficult life situation.

5. *Other Psychoses:*

a) *Schizophreniform Disorder*—schizophrenic disorder of short duration.
b) *Schizoaffective Disorder*—characterized by a mixture of schizophrenic symptoms (see #3 above) and a mood disturbance (see #6 below).
c) *Atypical Psychosis*—psychotic disorder that is not characterized by any of the previous descriptions.

6. *Affective Disorders:*

a) *Depressive Disorder, Single Episode*—characterized by a predominantly dysphoric mood or loss of interest and pleasure. It may also involve poor appetite and weight loss, inability to fall asleep or excessive sleep time, loss of energy, guilt feelings, feelings of self-reproach, inability to concentrate or recurrent morbid thoughts.
b) *Depressive Disorder, Recurrent*—characterized by repeated periods of dysphoric mood as described above.
c) *Bipolar Affective Disorder, Manic Phase*—characterized by a manic state (period of elevated, expansive or irritable mood as exemplified by accelerated psychomotor activity, flight of ideas, inflated self-esteem, reduced sleep time, inability to concentrate or extremely impulsive behavior) in an individual who has also suffered from depressive episodes.
d) *Bipolar Affective Disorder, Depressive Phase*—characterized as a depressive state in an individual who has also had manic episodes.

e) *Bipolar Affective Disorder, Mixed*—characterized by the existence of both manic and depressive states that alternate every few days.

f) *Cyclothymic Disorder*—characterized by the existence of both manic and depressive elements which are present at the same time and for a period of several years.

g) *Dysthymic Disorder*—depressive-like disorder that is not of sufficient severity or duration to be classified as a Depressive Disorder.

h) *Atypical Affective Disorder*—affective disorder that does not fit any of the descriptions given above.

7. *Anxiety Disorders:*

a) *Panic Disorder*—characterized by the occurrence of periods of extreme anxiety which are not the individual's response to a life threat or a phobic stimuli. The attacks may include any of the following: a breathing disturbance, palpitations, chest pain, choking sensations, dizziness, feelings of unreality, skin sensations, sweating, tremors or the fear of some impending danger.

b) *Generalized Anxiety Disorder*—characterized by the presence of an anxious mood which is not the individual's response to a significant environmental stress. The anxious mood may include tension, restlessness, tremors, fatigue, sweating, heart palpitations, stomach disturbances, apprehensiveness and worriness, irritability, insomnia or inability to concentrate.

c) *Obsessive Compulsive Disorder*—characterized by the presence of obsessions (disturbing and recurrent thoughts that the individual cannot get out of his mind) or compulsions (behaviors that the individual feels he has to carry out if he is to prevent some catastrophic event) which interfere with the normal functioning of the individual.

d) *Phobic Disorder*—characterized by the presence of an irrational fear and avoidance of an object or situation to a degree that interferes with the individual's normal functioning.

e) *Atypical Anxiety Disorder*—does not fit the descriptions of any of the disorders given above.

8. *Factitious Disorder:*

A Factitious Disorder is characterized by the production of psychological or physical symptoms that are under the control of the individuals and fulfill some emotional purpose in their lives.

9. Somatoform Disorders:

These disorders are characterized by the presence of somatic complaints that result from emotional factors alone and that do not appear to be under the control of the individual. Somatoform disorders include the following types:

a) *Psychogenic Pain Disorder*—involves only the complaint of pain.
b) *Conversion Disorder*—involves more than the complaint of pain in an individual who does not have the Somatization Disorder (see below).
c) *Somatization Disorder*—involves a life-long pattern of serious medical complaints so that the individual has a dramatic, vague and complicated medical history.
d) *Hypochondriacal Disorder*—characterized by unrealistic interpretations of normal sensations as indications of serious illness.
e) *Atypical Somatoform Disorder*—does not fit any of the types given above.

10. Dissociative Disorders:

a) *Psychogenic Amnesia*—characterized by the sudden inability to recall important personal information.
b) *Psychogenic Fugue*—characterized by a move to a new place of residence, an inability to recall one's past and an assumption of a new identity.
c) *Multiple Personality Disorder*—characterized by the existence of more than one distinct personality, each having a complex set of behaviors, memories, and social associations, and presenting a sudden transition from one personality to the other.
d) *Depersonalization Disorder*—characterized by an alteration in the individual's subjective experience of reality.

11. Gender Identity Disorders:

a) *Transsexualism*—characterized by a persistent discomfort with one's own sex and a wish to be a member of the opposite sex in the absence of physical or genetic abnormalities.
b) *Other Gender Identity Disorder*—characterized by a gender identity problem that does not fit the description given above.

12. Ego-Dystonic Homosexuality:

Ego-Dystonic Homosexuality is a disorder characterized by personal discomfort produced by a lack of interest in heterosexual activities and an attraction towards homosexuality.

13. Paraphilias:

This group of disorders is characterized by a disturbance of the sexual object so that the preferred method of sexual arousal involves the use of an unusual sexual stimulus.

a) *Zoophilia*—where animals are used to produce the sexual arousal.
b) *Pedophilia*—where children are used to produce the sexual arousal.
c) *Fetishism*—where nonliving objects are used to produce the sexual arousal.
d) *Exhibitionism*—where the sexual arousal is accomplished through the exposure of the genitals to unsuspecting strangers with whom no further activity is sought.
e) *Transvestism*—where the sexual arousal is accomplished through cross-dressing in a heterosexual male who does not have a gender identity disorder.
f) *Voyeurism*—where the sexual arousal is accomplished by looking at unsuspecting strangers when they are not fully dressed and with whom no further activity is sought.
g) *Sexual Masochism*—where the sexual arousal is accomplished through intentional participation in an activity in which the individual is physically harmed.
h) *Sexual Sadism*—where the sexual arousal is accomplished through intentional participation in an activity in which another individual is physically harmed.
i) *Atypical Paraphilia*—Paraphilia which does not fit any of the descriptions above.

14. Psychosexual Dysfunctions:

These disorders involve the persistent inability to obtain sexual fulfillment in cases where this disturbance is not symptomatic of another emotional disorder.

a) *Inhibited Sexual Desire*—characterized by a lack of sexual desire.

b) *Inhibited Sexual Excitement*—characterized by a lack of sexual excitement after an adequate sexual encounter and after experiencing sexual desire.
c) *Inhibited Sexual Orgasm*—characterized by an inability to reach a sexual orgasm after an adequate sexual encounter and after experiencing both sexual desire and excitement.
d) *Premature Ejaculation*—characterized by premature ejaculation due to the absence of reasonable voluntary control.
e) *Functional Dyspareunia*—characterized by the presence of pain during sexual intercourse.
f) *Functional Vaginismus*—characterized by the presence of involuntary spasms in the vagina that interfere with the sexual activity.
g) *Other Psychosexual Dysfunction*—sexual dysfunction different from any of the types described above.

15. Impulse Control Disorders:

These disorders are characterized by the inability to resist harmful impulses that are experienced as pleasurable in a case where this disturbance is not symptomatic of another emotional disorder.
a) *Pathological Gambling*—characterized by a preoccupation and urge to gamble.
b) *Kleptomania*—involves the impulse to steal where the pleasure is obtained from the act of stealing rather than from any material gain.
c) *Pyromania*—involves the urge to set fires where the pleasure obtained does not come from any practical gain for the individual.
d) *Isolated Explosive Disorder* or *Intermittent Explosive Disorder*—where the pleasure is obtained through violent and aggressive attacks in an individual who does not show impulsivity or anger outside of the explosive episodes and who feels guilty and contrite after the episodes.
e) *Other Impulse Control Disorder*—does not fit any of the description of the types given above.

II.E: REACTIVE DISORDERS

1. The Reactive Disorders are symptoms that appear at a time when the environmental situation is abnormally difficult. They may

represent either exaggerations of the basic personality style or symptoms that are added on to the basic personality style.

2. The Reactive Disorders may be classified in three groups as follows:
   a) Nonpsychotic symptoms resulting from a traumatic situation (a single catastrophic occurrence) and which are called Post-Traumatic Stress Disorders.
   b) Nonpsychotic symptoms resulting from any other kind of environmental stress are referred to as Adjustment Disorders.
   c) Psychotic symptoms resulting from environmental stresses are classified as Brief Reactive Psychoses.
3. The diagnoses in this group are not used when the presenting symptom is an exacerbation of an emotional disorder that was present prior to the onset of the stress.
4. In the descriptions that follow, the italicized terms are the official diagnoses used.

Descriptions

1. Post-Traumatic Stress Disorder:

The *Post-Traumatic Stress Disorder* develops after the occurrence of a traumatic event and is characterized by apathy, withdrawal or emotional constriction, together with recurrent recollections or dreams about the event. The disorder is considered *Acute* up to six months after the event and *Chronic* thereafter.

2. Adjustment Disorders:

These disorders are characterized by the appearance of symptomatology that is severe enough to impair the individual's social or occupational functioning and that is judged to be a reaction to an identifiable stressing situation. The Adjustment Disorders are classified as follows:

a) *Adjustment Disorder with Depressed Mood*
b) *Adjustment Disorder with Anxious Mood*
c) *Adjustment Disorder with Emotional Features*
d) *Adjustment Disorder with Physical Complaints*
e) *Adjustment Disorder with Disturbance of Conduct*

f) *Adjustment Disorder with Mixed Disturbance of Emotion and Conduct*
g) *Adjustment Disorder with Withdrawal*
h) *Other Adjustment Disorder*

3. Brief Reactive Psychosis:

This disorder is characterized by a brief period of incoherence, loosening of associations, delusions, hallucinations or disorganization of behavior appearing immediately following a stressing environmental situation.

II.F: CLINICAL SYNDROMES IN CHILDREN AND ADOLESCENTS

1. The syndromes presented in this section represent a mixed group with the only common denominator that they are seen in children. As a result, they include deficits due to organicity as with the mental retardations, impairments due to exaggerations or personality patterns as in the conduct disorders, as well as symptoms that are added on to the basic personality structure as with eating disorders.
2. Table 5 shows the basic classification scheme.
3. For help in treating childhood problems the reader may consult: Blanco, R. F. *Prescriptions for Children with Learning and Adjustment Problems*. Springfield, IL: Charles C. Thomas Publishing Co., 1972.
4. Further information about childhood syndromes can be obtained from the *DSM-III* or from B. B. Wolman (Ed.). *Manual of Child Psychopathology*. New York: McGraw-Hill, Inc., 1972.
5. In the descriptions that follow, the italicized terms are the official diagnoses used.
6. All of these disorders are coded on Axis I except for the Specific Developmental Disorders, which are coded on Axis II.

Descriptions

1. Mental Retardations:

These disorders are characterized by a significantly subaverage gen-

TABLE 5: Basic Classification Scheme for Children and Adolescents. Adapted from the *DSM-III* of the American Psychiatric Association. A group number is given to facilitate finding the syndrome in the pages that follow.

No.	*Disorder Group*	*Basic Characteristic*
1	Mental Retardation	Subaverage intellectual ability
2	Pervasive Developmental Disorders	Severe lack of overall development
3	Specific Developmental Disorders	Lack of development in specific area
4	Attention Deficit Disorders	Difficulty sustaining attention
5	Conduct Disorders	Presence of behavioral difficulties
6	Anxiety Disorders	Presence of marked anxiety
7	Eating Disorders	Disturbance of eating patterns
8	Stereotyped Movement Disorders	Presence of repetitive involuntary movements
9	Other Disorders of Childhood and Adolescence	

eral intellectual ability. They are classified according to levels as follows:

a) *Mild Mental Retardation*—IQ from 55 to 69.
b) *Moderate Mental Retardation*—IQ from 40 to 54.
c) *Severe Mental Retardation*—IQ from 25 to 39.
d) *Profound Mental Retardation*—IQ less than 25.
e) *Unspecified Mental Retardation*—IQ not available.

2. *Pervasive Developmental Disorders:*

These disorders are characterized by a severe lack of overall development in a child.

a) *Infantile Autism*—characterized by lack of responsiveness to other humans, bizarre behaviors and gross deficits in language development which were apparent from the time when the child was quite young.

b) *Atypical Childhood Psychosis*—characterized by an inability to form emotional relationships which was apparent when the child was still quite young. It may be accompanied by anxiety, inappropriate or rigid affect, changes in mood, repetitive or ritualistic behaviors, inactivity or hyperactivity, peculiar movement or postures, abnormality of speech, self-mutilation or a disturbance in the sensitivity to sensory stimuli.

3. *Specific Developmental Disorders:*

These disorders are characterized by a lack of development in one specific area of growth which is not due to inadequate learning opportunities or another physical or mental disorder (mental retardation has to be ruled out). The particular types are as follows:

a) *Developmental Reading Disorder*—characterized by a reading learning disability.
b) *Developmental Arithmetical Disorder*—characterized by an arithmetical learning disability.
c) *Developmental Receptive Language Disorder*—characterized by a learning disability of language comprehension.
d) *Developmental Expressive Language Disorder*—characterized by an expressive language disability in an individual who has acceptable receptive language.
e) *Developmental Articulation Disorder*—characterized by a misarticulation of speech sounds.
f) *Other Specific Developmental Disorder*—Specific Developmental Disorder that is different from those described above.

4. *Attention Deficit Disorder:*

The *Attention Disorder Deficit Disorder* is characterized by a difficulty sustaining attention and may be accompanied by impulsivity, low frustration tolerance, or hyperactivity.

5. *Conduct Disorders:*

Conduct disorders are characterized by the presence of substantial behavioral difficulties. They include:

a) *Undersocialized Conduct Disorder*—characterized by a lack of acceptance of any loyalty or responsibility towards others and an attempt to set up relationships in which others are exploited for personal benefit. It may also be accompanied by aggressiveness and hostility towards others.

b) *Socialized Conduct Disorder*—characterized by criminal behavior or physical aggressiveness in an individual who is capable of interpersonal loyalty and does not attempt to exploit others.

6. *Anxiety Disorders:*

These are disorders in which the predominant symptom is the presence of anxiety. Three types are presently recognized:

a) *Separation Anxiety Disorder*—characterized by persistent fears that something bad would happen if the child were separated from his family.
b) *Avoidant Disorder*—characterized by persistent shyness that is severe enough to interfere with the individual's ability to function with his peers in an individual who has warm and satisfying relationships with family members.
c) *Overanxious Disorder*—characterized by persistent worrying about future events.

7. *Eating Disorders:*

Eating disorders are characterized by some disturbance in the child's eating behavior. The different types follow:

a) *Anorexia Nervosa*—characterized by a fear of becoming obese together with some disturbance of body image and significant weight loss. The weight loss is due to either refusal to eat appropriate amounts of food or self-induced vomiting.
b) *Bulimia*—characterized by binges during which large amounts of food are consumed in a short period of time together with fears of lack of control over this impulse.
c) *Pica*—characterized by the ingestion of nonedible substances.
d) *Rumination*—characterized by self-induced vomiting with resulting weight loss in an individual who does not have anorexia nervosa.
e) *Atypical Eating Disorder*—not characterized by any of the above.

8. *Stereotyped Movement Disorders:*

These disorders are characterized by the presence of repetitive and involuntary movements which can be voluntarily suppressed for some periods of time, and which are not symptomatic of another childhood disorder. They include:

a) *Tic Disorder* (can be *Transient* or *Chronic*)
b) *Tourette's Disorder*—consists of multiple vocal tics.
c) *Other Stereotyped Movement Disorder*—not described above (e.g., head banging, rocking, hand movements, etc.)

9. *Other Disorders of Childhood and Adolescence:*

a) *Reactive Attachment Disorder of Infancy*—develops after a gross lack of care for the infant and is characterized by a lack of development of social responsiveness (e.g., lack of visual tracking of faces, no smiling). The disorder is accompanied by a withdrawn existence (e.g., weak cry, excessive sleep) and weight loss. The diagnosis is used only in cases where the disturbance is not due to another disorder.
b) *Schizoid Disorder of Childhood and Adolescence*—characterized by a lack of interest in relating with peers and an avoidance of social contacts in an individual who does not show a Pervasive Developmental Disorder.
c) *Elective Mutism*—characterized by a continuous and persistent refusal to speak to most other persons in cases where the refusal is not symptomatic of another disorder.
d) *Oppositional Disorder*—characterized by pervasive and persistent oppositional, negativistic and provocative behaviors in an individual who does not show a Pervasive Developmental Disorder or a Conduct Disorder.
e) *Identity Disorder*—disorder of late adolescence characterized by a subjective distress over uncertainty about self-identity, self-goals, etc.
f) *Stuttering*
g) *Functional Enuresis*—characterized by a persistent involuntary voiding of urine.
h) *Functional Encopresis*—characterized by a persistent involuntary voiding of feces.
i) *Sleep Walking Disorder*—characterized by arising from bed and walking with a blank facial expression. The episode is accompanied by amnesia, abnormal electrical brain activity and some disorientation upon awakening.

j) *Sleep Terror Disorder*—characterized by an abrupt awakening in a state of intense anxiety which may be accompanied by confusion, disorientation and perseverative motor movements. The disorder is accompanied by normal electric brain activity.

III Diagnostic Methods

III.A: THE DIAGNOSTIC INTERVIEW

1. Some therapists assume that the treatment for every patient will consist of basically the same maneuver. If this is the case, the type of diagnostic interview about to be described will not be needed. However, the assumption that treatment will always take the same form does not seem appropriate with many patients and in many clinical settings. Different clients come with different problems, goals for treatment, and abilities to change.
2. The purpose of the diagnostic interview described here is to *gather information about the client*. The working assumption is that treatment interventions are premature since the interviewer does not know enough about the client to determine what kind of intervention will be beneficial.
3. Two aspects of the diagnostic interview will be discussed:
   a) The content—the actual information that is needed from the patient—as well as the examiner's evaluation of the patient's psychological functioning (mental status).
   b) The method or process through which the information is obtained.
4. The information obtained from the patient should include:
   a) The Presenting Complaint—what problems the patient is having, how long s/he has had these problems and why is s/he having them now.
   b) A Mental Health History—what emotional problems the patient has had in the past; what treatment, if any, was received and how the problems were resolved.
   c) The Present Life Situation—where does the patient live and with whom; how are the relationships of the different members of the household; where does s/he work and his/her

income bracket; how does s/he relate to coworkers and what problems, if any, s/he is having on the job.

d) Childhood History—a brief account of the family of origin and the major events of his/her childhood.

e) Educational and Occupational History—the extent of education and training together with the kind of jobs obtained.

f) Social History—Relationships that the patient has had throughout life; marriages, divorces, etc.

5. The clinical observations of the patient during the diagnostic interview together with the content information obtained should be sufficient to evaluate most aspects of the mental status of the patient. The reader should see Section III.B for further information about the mental status evaluation.

6. The tactic used for the interview is to prompt the patient to talk about an area of his/her life with a general, open-ended question (e.g., "How can I help you?" "Could you tell me a little bit about your family?" etc.). The advantage of the general, open-ended question is that:

a) It does not take time away from the patient with lengthy questions by the interviewer.

b) It gives the control of the interview to the patient so that s/he has a chance to demonstrate how s/he functions. The patient will then organize the answers in his/her unique way, giving clues about personality style, level of pathology, preoccupations, etc.

c) It allows the patient to choose the areas that s/he is most concerned with.

7. If the patient stops talking before an area is covered, further promptings may be appropriate. These may take the form of:

a) Silence, giving the patient time to think and continue the narrative.

b) An encouraging gesture like a nod, a "yes" or something similar.

c) A verbal request for more information like, "Go on, please" or "Could you tell me more about that?" etc.

d) A reflective statement that echoes what the patient has said, usually underlying the feelings involved like, "You felt hurt when your girlfriend forgot your birthday."

e) A summary statement like, "Up to now you have told me the difficulties that you are having at work. Can you tell me more about your life?"
f) An interpretation like, "You seem to want to avoid talking about this. I wonder what your feelings are about sharing it with me."
g) A statement of support or reassurance, in the case of a fearful or uneasy patient.
h) A confrontation like, "The judge told you that you had to see me, but you really don't want to talk to me."
i) A self-disclosure which may be used when a patient is really afraid of revealing him or herself in a sensitive area and when an honest sharing of the interviewer's own life would make the patient feel less vulnerable.

The goal of this type of assistance is only to encourage further disclosure. As a result, the less intensive a prompting is, the more appropriate it would be. Readers are, therefore, encouraged to use most frequently the first few (silences, encouraging gestures, etc.). Statements of support, confrontations and self-disclosures should be used infrequently and only after other attempts have failed.

8. There are times, however, when the interviewer should switch from the open-ended questions to more specific ones. This switch is particularly appropriate when:
a) The patient appears lost with the more general prompting and needs more guidance.
b) It has already been established that the patient handles the general, open-ended questions by giving tangential or irrelevant answers that do not add further information.
c) The patient has already covered an area but has left out some details that the interviewer sees as important.

These specific questions should be asked in a direct and clear manner but without suggesting answers to the patient.

9. In some extreme cases of confused or noninsightful patients, even direct, specific questions do not bring out the information wanted. In some occasions, then, the use of a multiple choice questioning technique is appropriate. Some patients are then able to pick the choice they feel answers the question.

10. After an area has been covered, the interviewer should switch to a new area, usually using again the more general and open-ended questioning technique.

11. The chart shown on Figure 3 maps out the proposed plan for a diagnostic interview.

12. The following events are to be avoided since they usually do not lead to a productive information gathering system:
    a) Questions that antagonize the patient.
    b) Questions that provide an answer. It is better to ask "How were you feeling?" than "Were you feeling nervous?"
    c) "Machine gunning" (asking one direct question after another and giving the patient little time to respond).
    d) Prolonged silences.
    e) A situation where the patient is allowed to go on talking while the interviewer is not paying attention.
    f) Any situation that makes the patient feel ill at ease, shame, embarrassment, rejection, etc.

13. The reader is referred to Section IV.E for a review of general difficult situations in handling patients. There are, however, some difficult situations that are specific to the interview. These include:
    a) The overtalkative patient
    b) The nontalker
    c) The confused or incoherent patient
    d) The tangential or circumstantial patient

14. With the *overtalkative* patient the following suggestions may be useful:
    a) Share the task that you have to accomplish with the patient (getting information about the patient in quite a number of areas in a short period of time). Try to enlist the patient's help so that it becomes a collaborative enterprise in which s/he is also involved.
    b) As you learn more about the patient, an interpretation can be attempted: Does he talk more when he is anxious? Does she talk more when discussing a particular area of her life situation? etc. This approach can be followed with interpretations when the patient starts talking excessively again.

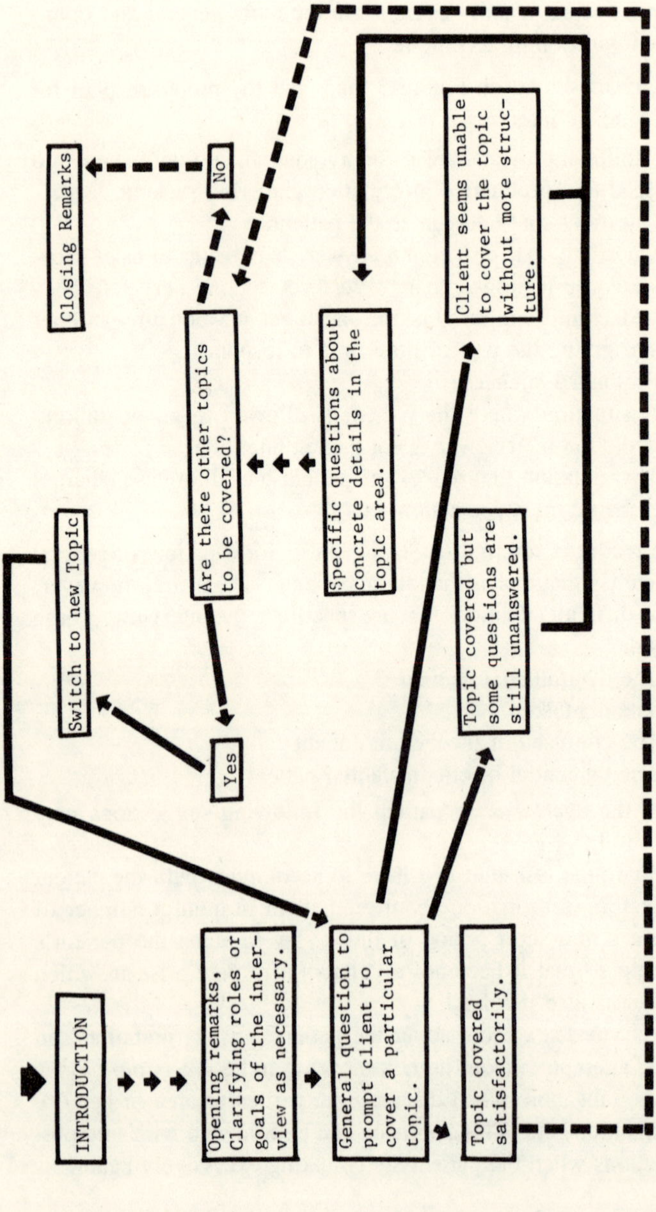

Figure 3. Proposed Flow Chart for Diagnostic Interviews. Adapted from Richard Greenblatt (unpublished work).

c) Reinforce the patient by demonstrating your appreciation when s/he gives a concise answer.

15. With the *nontalker* the trick is usually to figure out why the patient does not talk. Likely options may be:
    a) Extreme fear or confusion.
    b) Paranoid suspiciousness.
    c) Anger—this is particularly likely when the person feels forced to meet with the interviewer.
    d) An organic impairment.

    The cause of the lack of communication may be determined by:
    a) Spending some time with the patient.
    b) Asking the patient why s/he doesn't want to talk. Maybe, some interpretations can be tentatively suggested if s/he does not respond.
16. The *confused* patient can be helped by asking questions that call for short and concrete answers.
17. The *tangential* or circumstantial patient may be handled using the same suggestions presented for the overtalkative patient (#14 above).
18. When a report of the diagnostic interview is needed, it can be written following the outline presented under #4 above. A write-up of the diagnostic interview given as an example can be found as the example of a data base write-up in Section VI.A.
19. For examiner behaviors useful during a diagnostic interview see Section IV.D. Good references for further reading which include examples are:

    R. E. Froelich and F. M. Bishop, *Clinical Interviewing Skills*. St. Louis: C. V. Mosby Co., 1977.

    R. A. MacKinnon and R. Michels, *The Psychiatric Interview in Clinical Practice*. Philadelphia: Saunders, 1971.

Example of a Diagnostic Interview

I: Hello. I am ——. How can I help you? P: Well, I don't know. A lot of strange things are going on and stuff without the. . . . I was with this, I was the last few months . . . I've been hearing people tell	*The interview starts with a brief, serious and professional tone. The opening*

me that I must be crazy, I must be a nut. So after two weeks went by, I decided to come into the hospital. It seemed strange to me that at one time everything I was doing struck me as though somebody was making notes or notations of it and then, in an indirect way, like a third person, they would be talking to one another and I would be the third person but I would hear what was being said and I could relate to what they were talking about but yet, they would vary the conversation to the extent that they would talk about different people or different places. When they came right down to the subject of whatever it is that they were talking about, it would be a completely different subject all together but yet it was something that I could associate with or relate to.

question is very general. The tone throughout the interview is one of warmth and understanding.

Patient shows:

1. *Ideas of reference*
2. *Feelings of depersonalization*
3. *Confusion about himself*
4. *Inability to express himself with clarity*

I: Had this ever happened to you before?
P: No.

Interviewer questions about past emotional disturbances.

I: How old are you?
P: Twenty-four.
I: So about two months ago you started feeling that strange things were happening.

Interviewer needs age in order to place information in perspective. Then he gets patient back to talking about the presenting complaint—with a general prompting.

P: Well, that took . . . three or four months ago. Yes. I don't know what really is behind it all, other than the fact that I was told that if I can't find out through the people who I'm with, I might as well go to the hospital and let them tell me what's wrong and they could probably, they would be able to straighten out the situation and tell me what's going on.

I: What about prior to this time? Have you ever thought of yourself as needing help for some emotional problem?

Interviewer inquires again about past mental health problems. (Given the degree of pathology, he finds it hard to believe that P. has never received treatment before).

P: No.

I: Have you ever seen a psychiatrist or a psychologist before?

P: No, I haven't . . not a psychiatrist . . . I mean I may have talked to an analyst and not really been aware of it and yet . . . when I did come to Chicago myself, I had a rather difficult time trying to establish whom I was talking to. I came here looking for one of two things—a police officer or a priest, and nobody wanted to identify with one or another, nobody wanted to be one or the other.

Patient continues to show confusion and tangentiality of thought.

I: When was it that you came to Chicago?

Interviewer moves into recent past.

P: Roughly three months ago?

I: What were you doing before?

P: I was in Michigan in the U.P. which is the Upper Peninsula. I messed around and expired or used up all of my, what do you call it? . . . unemployment. So I ended up looking for three jobs, work at —— [store], working at a factory area of —— [same store] and I can't recall working at where else, while I was there in Michigan. I do

Patient has not had stable employment for some time.

remember the time when I traveled downstate for two hours, where my folks are, where I completed high school, and I went through the employment officer and got a job through them working as a painter. I was painting there. They were working under contract work and I was working as a painter myself. I painted the roof and the pipes that were up there. I don't know, something like 45 feet, 50 feet, up above, 50 feet off the ground.

I: Where are your parents from?
P: This is —— [state].
I: And when did you leave home?
P: When I went into the service.
I: How old were you then?
P: About nineteen.
I: How long did you spend in the service?
P: Three years, 11 months and 20 some odd days.
I: (Laughing) You got 'em all counted up! How was it?

Interviewer continues to move into the patient's past history. First he uses some specific questions to place the information in perspective, but he soon asks a general question regarding the service and allows the patient to go on.

P: I really didn't enjoy it. I didn't enjoy seeing all the things I saw going on and I was anxiously waiting to get out. I knew I had a four year commitment and I didn't think I would attain the benefits that I would receive if I went about and took an early out. They tried twice and on their second attempt they managed to put me out by at least eight days early. Something happened to their paper work and they didn't succeed the first time so they put it through again the second time.

The patient shows uncertain and unsystematized paranoid thinking.

I: Did they kick you out?

The interviewer

P: No, I received an honorable discharge.

I: After finishing your time?

P: Yes.

I: So, what's this about managing to get you out before your time?

P: That's rather strange. I would say some of the individuals in there didn't really care for me, some of the people who were in the position of authority. I know that at one time, one of my supervisors who I got along with had a favorable attitude towards me. His supervisor didn't particularly care for me, who was a civilian. When I got out of the service, I was an equipment operator, that was the last job I performed while I was in the service. He was a civilian and he didn't really object to me and in fact he, I had the impression that he was really trying to help me as best he could. But he worked under a civilian who really didn't care one way or the other. He was out to do his job. His senior, this superior, was a major and I had the impression that he didn't particularly care for the major, in his branch. His superior was a lieutenant colonel, again, he was doing his job.

I: So what did they gain by putting you out?

P: Well, stopping my ideals, my attitudes, my thoughts. Because, see what they did is, they took me from my job, my working situation, and because they couldn't put anything on me, or nail me with anything, they, and they didn't have any solid reason for just putting me out of the service, they put me in a situation and an environment where I had very little exposure to people. They put me in an equipment crib, I recognized this to be a made-up job. I had to record in a simple

asks some specific questions in order to clarify what actually happened.

The patient responds in a tangential manner and shows great uncertainty. The paranoid ideation is, nevertheless, indisputable.

notebook paper who was taking out shovels and equipment. The paper was not regulation form, was simple stationary.

I: And this was the job that they put you to do because they didn't like you, wanted to stop your ideals and wanted to get rid of you.

P: Yes, this is the job they gave me to do until my time ran out.

I: So, after you finished, then what happened?

The interviewer questions the patient in order to fill the gap between the service time and the recent past.

P: I moved downtown. I went to the nearest city in Michigan and put in an application to do some type of work. Then, when I realized that I wasn't going to get any job, I realized that the next best thing for me to do was to leave the area and look for work elsewhere.

I: Where did you go?

P: Here.
(Brief silence)

I: But, in the meantime, you were able to work for —— [store].

P: I worked one day! My part time jobs never consisted of two or three days. The longest job I held was when I decided to go home, down in —— [state], and I worked from the 27th of December until the 3rd of January. I was making $6.20/hr. I imagine that that was because of the holidays. I said $2.20/hr, isn't that what I said? Wait a minute, $2.50 an hour? . . . I don't even remember what it was!
(Brief silence)

The patient clarifies the job issue. The impression now is that he has been functioning very poorly and has been unable to hold on to the jobs that he was able to acquire.

I: Tell me a little bit about your family.

P: About my family?

I: Uh hum.

The interviewer shifts the topic in order to get at the family background.

P: Well, I rather not talk about my family, you know, being it that it is recorded because . . . all I would say is that our family, we don't see eye-to-eye, we don't get along. . . .

The patient objects at first but then goes on.

I: Who's at home?

P: My parents, and I have two sisters, they are younger than I am.
(Brief silence)

I: And you had trouble getting along with all of them?

P: Well, my own opinion is that my father was harder on me because I was older and he gave in to my youngest sister because he treated her as the baby of the family.
(Brief silence)

The interviewer returns with specific questions in order to get some specific information that is needed.

I: So, when you went into the service, things were not going well at home.

P: No. I went into the service to get away and make a life on my own. It seems like things didn't go well at all. I went in to make a 20-year career out of it but things didn't go well at all.

I: How come?

P: How come? I imagine that it has to do with the people I became involved with and associated with while I was in service. I imagine, I am not really sure. It seems like someone was always having a turn or a play about what was going on with my life.

The interviewer sees a chance to tap, once more, into the events that took place in the Army. This turns out to be wasted time since the patient returns to the paranoid ideas.

I: Have you ever been in the hospital before?

P: I was treated a few times, yes.

I: What was the problem?

The interviewer now returns to questions dealing with past emotional problems.

P:	Well, the most distinctive time I recall was ah, a brain scan, something that took place after I cross-trained. See, when I first enlisted I went into a career field known as a "weapons mechanic" which is nothing more than a "bomb jockey" better known as a "bomb loader." I loaded weapons in aircraft, and I got into problems with the law in relations to marijuana, and through that, it took place four or five months after I got to —— [military base] and that situation brought about a change in my career status. They pointed out that I had the option of getting out of the service or cross-training. I selected three different jobs that I wanted to go into, now that I couldn't be a weapons mechanic because what they found in my car was 12.5 grams of marijuana which is nearly estimated as enough to roll two joints. This was the evidence of the crime of what I considered my friend, he placed it in my car instead of sticking it in his pocket and when they searched the car, that's what they found. And, in spite of the fact that it was his, because it was in my car, I received credit for it. I was held for being in possession of it.	*The patient admits some trouble this time but is clearly very defensive about it. (It was later found that there were several psychiatric admissions while in service.) An incident involving a drug charge is then narrated.*
I:	Do you take drugs?	*The interviewer asks specific questions to rule out the possibility of drug abuse. The patient makes some denials but it is obvious by now that the patient may be unreliable.*
P:	No. I used to smoke pot a long time ago.	
I:	Only pot?	
P:	Yes.	
I:	And when was the last time you smoked it?	
P:	Two . . . no. About four or five months ago. (Brief silence)	

I: I noticed that you are carrying a Bible. Are you a pretty religious fellow?

The interviewer moves into yet another area through an observation that is followed by a general question.

P: No. I am not a very religious fella. I turn to the Bible because it reveals many things to me. I found that the situation I'm in is not totally of my own doing. I realize that I was goaded into a situation where it doesn't matter which way I go. It reminds me a little bit of the service. All the alternatives have been considered and all the objectives for any alternative have been ruled out. Now, as a weak Bible believer or a weak person . . . and the faith of god . . . what will occur is once again this . . . it isn't the first time that I pick up the Bible and read it following out what may be considered a weak Bible believer. What will occur next is for me to start backsliding, more or less meaning that I will regress back into the same old rut or the same plot or position I was at.

The response shows:

1) *Ideas of reference?*
2) *Paranoid feelings, perhaps towards the interviewer*
3) *A schizophrenic, confused flavor to the religiosity (the "weak Bible believer" idea)*
4) *An insight? (Religiosity is associated with backsliding).*

I: OK. Unfortunately, we have to stop at this time. What I would like to do is arrange for you to come into the hospital. We, then, would have more time to talk about some of these issues and figure out in what ways we can be of help to you. How do you feel about that idea?

At this point arrangements are made to continue the evaluation and treatment and the interview is closed.

P: That's all right.

I: Good. I am going to have you wait outside while I do some of the paper work. I enjoyed talking to you today and I wanted to thank you for allowing me to record the interview.

P: OK. Thank you (walking out).

III.B: THE MENTAL STATUS EVALUATION

The Mental Status Evaluation involves an assessment of how the patient is functioning psychologically. This assessment is usually done in the course of a diagnostic interview (see Section III.A), although information obtained from other sources may be included. The areas of assessment are:

1. Appearance: Physical characteristics, the formality and appropriateness of the patient's clothes, cleanliness, etc.
2. Relationship with the Examiner: Was the patient comfortable and open or was he evasive, distant, aloof, suspicious, nervous, etc.?
3. Evaluation of Intellect
   a) Orientation—does the patient know where he is, the time and date, who you are and who he is?
   b) Coherence and clearness of thought—can the patient express himself clearly, is he confused or demented etc.?
   c) Approximate intellectual ability.
   d) Evidence of intellectual impairment—does the patient have a lot of trouble understanding instructions, etc.? Occasionally an attempt is made to test this more formally by using a proverb and asking the patient to explain what it means or using some math problem that the patient is asked to resolve. The present author does not encourage this technique since the attempts are often very inadequate. If there is any doubt regarding the intellectual integrity of the patient, formal testing should be done (see Section III. E).
   e) Evidence of memory impairment—can the patient remember recent and past events? This is another area that may be assessed more formally, (see note under 3d above).
4. Evaluation of Thought Process: Evidence of loose associa-

tions, bizarreness, delusions, hallucinations, preoccupations, poor judgment or obsessions should be noted.

5. Evaluation of Affective Response
   a) Appropriateness—is the emotional response in keeping with the content of the conversation?
   b) Prevailing mood—happy, sad, worried, etc.
6. Anxiety Level: Note the way in which the patient handles the anxiety, defense mechanisms, etc.
7. Motor Activity
   a) Posture, manner of walking, tremors, gestures, tics, etc.
   b) Activity level—over or underactive
   c) Speech—rate of flow, loudness, pronunciation difficulties, etc.
8. An example of a write-up of a mental status exam can be found in Section VI.A. Books recommended for further reading are:

   Pruyser, P. W. *The Psychological Examination: A Guide for Clinicians*. New York: International Universities Press, 1979.

   Strub, R. and Black, F. *The Mental Status Examination in Neurology*. Philadelphia: F. A. Davis, 1977.

III.C: INTRODUCTION TO PSYCHOMETRICS

1. Most typically, the use of psychometric methods involves two tasks:
   a) The obtaining of information through psychological tests.
   b) The sharing of this information with other professionals.
2. The method used for obtaining information depends mostly on the purpose of the evaluation. Four general areas will be considered:
   a) School Testing—intellectual evaluation of children in order to recommend placement and methods for remediation.
   b) Testing for Organicity—intellectual evaluation of individuals (mostly adults) in order to determine if there is an impairment of intellectual functioning that could be due to brain damage.
   c) Emotional Evaluation—evaluation of personality dynamics, situational factors and level of functioning of an individual.
   d) Vocational Testing—evaluation of ability, interests and per-

sonality aspects of an individual in order to counsel with regards to vocational choice and training.

Further coverage of these areas will be found in the sections that follow.

3. The sharing of information is accomplished mainly through the psychological report. The following are general suggestions:
   a) The report should be professional but also interesting and readable. Where the line is drawn between these is a matter of personal judgment. Facts about the client's life, quotes from the client's responses and changes in sentence structure can be used to make the report enjoyable. However, it is usually felt that jokes, extraneous anecdotes or similar gimmicks give an unprofessional flavor.
   b) The report should be well organized. Each paragraph should cover an easily identifiable issue. The shift from issue to issue should be rational and orderly.
   c) The report should be appropriate, containing all the information that could be of use but without burdening the reader with information that he or she already has, or with trivial details.
4. A reference on writing reports is:
   Tallent, N. *Psychological Report Writing*. Englewood Cliffs, NJ: Prentice Hall, Inc., 1976.
5. More specific suggestions will be made in the sections that follow, where each of the four areas of evaluation is treated individually. In each case, some preliminary comments are made, followed by a report outline only, with the expectation that the student will alter it substantially whenever appropriate.
6. Many psychological tests will be noted in the chapters that follow. A thorough discussion of each test is beyond the scope of the present book. The reader is referred to the yearbook below which lists every test that is commercially available, gives a critical description of the instrument, presents a comprehensive list of references, and cites the retail source: Buros, O. K. (Ed.) *The Eighth Mental Measurement Yearbook*. Highland Park, NJ: Gryphon Press, 1978.

III.D: SCHOOL TESTING

1. School testing typically involves an intellectual evaluation of children in order to recommend a placement and method of remediation. An interview of at least one member of the family and the teacher is usually necessary.
2. It is advisable to do an intellectual evaluation even when the complaint is behavioral. Children that have undiagnosed intellectual impairments may find the school situation frustrating and show nonadaptive behaviors as a result.
3. The usual strategy consists of administering a general test battery, later following up the low scores with similar tests not included in the original battery. Typically the general battery includes a Wechsler test (Wechsler Pre-School and Primary Scale of Intelligence or the Wechsler Intelligence Scale for Children—now revised) in addition to one or two quick tests (Draw-a-Person, Bender Gestalt, the Visual Motor Integration Test, or the Peabody Picture Vocabulary Test).
4. In the absence of information from the teacher regarding the pupil's academic level, an achievement test (Peabody Individual Achievement Test, Wide Range Achievement Test) should also be administered.
5. A good textbook for further background on testing children is: Sattler, J. M. *Assessment of Children's Intelligence,* Philadelphia: W. B. Saunders Co., 1974.
6. Table 6 presents a nonexhaustive list of school diagnoses and diagnostic indicators. Further help can be obtained from: Bush, W. J. and Waugh, K. W. *Diagnosing Learning Disabilities.* Columbus, OH: Charles E. Merrill Publishing Co., 1976.

Report Outline

1. The Referral Problem:

Difficulties that the child has which have been previously noted. Rationale for further assessment and the kind of information that is needed.

2. Family History (usually obtained through interview):

TABLE 6: List of School Diagnoses and Diagnostic Indicators

"Diagnosis"	*Function Impaired*	*IQ Estimate on the Basis of Unimpaired (Higher Scores)*	*Examples of Typical Tests that May Be Showing Impairment**
None	None	Above 80	
Behavioral Disorder	Emotional		Rorschach, TAT, Children's Apperception Test, Blacky Pictures
None ("Bilingual")	Language		Vocabulary, ITPA's Grammatic Closure, Auditory Closure, Verbal Expression. To lesser degree: Comprehension, Information, Similarities, ITPA's Auditory subtests.
"Cultural Deprivation"	Knowledge of Culture		Comprehension, Information
Language Disability	Language		Vocabulary, ITPA's Grammatic Closure, Auditory Closure, Verbal Expression. To lesser degree: Comprehension, Information, Similarities, ITPA's Auditory subtests.
Learning Disability	Spatio-visual		Block Design, Object Assembly, Raven's Progressive Matrices.
Learning Disability	Motor-visual		Bender Gestalt, VMI, Coding, Mazes, Frostig's Test of Visual Perception
Learning Disability	Memory Attention Span		Wechsler Memory Scale, Digit Span, Benton Visual Retention Test, ITPA's Visual Sequential Memory.
Speech Impairment	Pronunciation		
Educable Mental Retardation	All intellectual functions	Between 55 and 80	All intellectual tests
Trainable Mental Retardation	All intellectual functions	Below 55	All intellectual tests

*When not otherwise indicated, the subtests used are from the Wechsler Intelligence Scale for Children (WISC-R). ITPA refers to the Illinois Test of Psycholinguistic Abilities.

a) Parental Background—types of families of origin, social history prior to present marriage, age at time of marriage, etc.
b) Educational and Occupational History of Parents
c) Siblings—names, ages, activities in which they are involved.
d) Present Relationships in Family—how parents relate to each other and to the children, how child relates to other family members, interpersonal problems present.

3. *Developmental History:*

a) Difficulties with respect to the child during pregnancy or birth.
b) Discussion of developmental milestones—development of language, walking and motor abilities, toilet training, weaning, etc.
c) Medical problems or injuries.

4. *School History:*

List all schools attended, period of attendance, levels of achievement, problems noted at earlier times.

5. *Behavioral Observations:*

a) Appearance (can be omitted when all readers will know the child or when it is unremarkable).
b) Description of examiner-client interaction.
c) General behavior—comments made, unusual behavior, etc.
d) Specific Test Behavior—motivation, attitude toward testing, etc.

6. *Test Scores*

7. *Discussion of Test Scores:*

a) Two levels of conceptualization or distance away from actual scores may be possible:
   (1) One step removed from actual scores would be a conceptualization dealing with the specific abilities in which the client excels or has difficulties. An example would be stating that a child who scores low on the Bender Gestalt and the VMI has a visual-motor problem.
   (2) Two steps removed from the actual scores would be a conceptualization that groups the specific abilities and provides a rationale for their being high or low. An example would

be a child who did poorly on verbal subtests and culture-related tasks where these deficiencies can be explained on the basis of foreign background. Needless to say, it is impossible to conceptualize the test scores at this level in every case.

b) Emotional, social or family aspects that may be affecting the intellectual functioning should also be discussed.

8. *Recommendations:*

a) Two types of recommendations should be included:
  (1) Placement recommendations
  (2) Treatment recommendations

b) The placement recommendations should be made, keeping in mind the options available in the particular school district. Options often available are:
  (1) The "regular" classroom
  (2) The "slow" classroom
  (3) The bilingual classroom (for children for whom English is not the native language)
  (4) Title I program (for children who are "culturally deprived" so that they have not had the chance to learn as much as their peers)
  (5) Learning Disability Tutoring (where the child is kept in the regular room except for a certain period during the day)
  (6) Learning Disability Classroom (LD)
  (7) Language Learning Disability Classroom (LLD) (a subspeciality of the LD category)
  (8) Speech therapy
  (9) Behavioral Disability Classroom (BD) (for children with emotional or discipline problems)
  (10) Educable Mentally Handicap Room (EMH)
  (11) Trainable Mentally Handicap Room (TMH)

c) The placement recommendation should be biased towards the less severe (uppermost) alternative in cases where some doubt exists.

d) The treatment recommendation should deal with specific ways of counteracting the area of difficulty. A good reference book is: Blanco, R. F. *Prescriptions for Children with Learning and Adjustment Problems,* Springfield, Illinois: Charles C. Thomas, 1972.

9. A Summary

Report Example

Name:	John Fernandez
Birthdate:	6/16/69
Teacher:	Ms. Jones, 1st grade
School:	Lincoln School, Chicago, IL
Referred by:	Ms. Green, School Social Worker

Referral Problem:

John is markedly behind the other first graders. He cannot count past the first few numbers, cannot copy his name, is very distractible and has a very primitive vocabulary.

Family History:

Mrs. Fernandez was interviewed as part of the evaluation. She is a 27-year-old white woman. Although she is overweight, she remains pleasant looking. She carried her youngest child who is only two months old and who was asleep for most of the session. The examiner felt that she was at ease and related in an open manner with him, giving as much information as she could in response to questions.

Mrs. Fernandez was born in Mexico but immigrated to the States when she was only two years old. She lived in Texas most of her life. At the age of 18, after her schooling was finished, she came to Illinois to live with her brother and sister-in-law. This home situation presented some problems since Mrs. Fernandez felt that her sister-in-law did not like her and was constantly abusing her. As a result, when her first husband proposed to her, she accepted, even though she did not have much admiration or affection for him. They were quickly married and John was conceived.

It was within the same year of the marriage, at the age of 18, that Mrs. Fernandez separated from her first husband. The incident that brought this about was the poor health of the child's maternal grandmother. The grandmother, who lived in Texas, had become blind and needed someone to care for her. Mrs. Fernandez' husband did not want to go South and told her that she had to choose between her mother and him. Mrs. Fernandez chose her mother and left. Although the mother died shortly thereafter, Mrs. Fernandez never bothered to return and eventually filed for a divorce.

Three years later Mrs. Fernandez married her present husband. He is 39-years-old and works at a farm. Although he was born in Texas, his family had originally come from Mexico. Mr. Fernandez was also married before and has four children from the previous marriage. There are two children that were born from this present marriage—Shirley who is four and presently attending kindergarten and Eddie, the two-month-old baby.

According to Mrs. Fernandez, she gets along very well with her husband. He is very interested in the children and treats John like his own son.

Mrs. Fernandez does not know of any other member of the family who had severe difficulties in school. According to her, her daughter Shirley is doing well, but the school already had some concerns regarding her. In general, the impression was that the family tended to be poorly educated and intellectually limited.

Apparently both Mr. and Mrs. Fernandez are bilingual and both languages are spoken at home. She feels, nevertheless, that John can function better in Spanish than in English.

Developmental History:

John was the product of an uncomplicated pregnancy. His birth, however, took place after 12 hours of labor and as a result of a Caesarean section. John has not had serious medical problems but tends to get "bronchitis" or chest colds often.

Mrs. Fernandez speaks with some feeling regarding John's difficulties in learning to talk. He was already three years old and he was not able to speak one single word. The mother blames herself for some of this retardation since she used to get him what he wanted without forcing him to use a word to ask for it. Her second husband started to criticize her after a while for this attitude, and she then would force John to say the word "water" or whatever before she would get it for him. With this system he has been able to learn what most common things are called and to use these words appropriately. John, however, never uses sentences and tends to confine himself to simple nouns.

A few years ago, when the family was still in Texas, it was thought that John was hyperactive. After a medical evaluation he was put on some medication which seemed effective in controlling his activity level. Last May, when the family moved to Illinois, the medication was discontinued. According to his mother, the hyperactivity has returned, but she is afraid of possible long-term effects of the medication and has chosen to let it go for the time being.

Mrs. Fernandez is concerned with the way that John relates to other children. She feels that he usually seeks kids who are older than he is and sets up a relationship in which his friends physically abuse him. He never fights back and frequently comes home crying after being beaten up. Mrs. Fernandez has tried unsuccessfully to persuade John to find friends who are closer to his own age or, at least, to fight back. Also, their complaints to the parents of the older children have been to no avail.

Behavioral Observations:

At first John was extremely shy but seemed comfortable with the examiner, not showing any signs of anxiety. He appeared to understand the examiner's Spanish but was extremely nonverbal, responding with his head whenever possible and only verbalizing single words when completely necessary. He knew a certain number of nouns but never used them in a sentence or even with articles or prepositions. Although some difficulties in pronunciation were noted, these difficulties seemed minor in the light of the primitive level of language development.

John was also unable to understand instructions of any complexity. He is obedient and followed well any simple command. He was able to establish an emotional rapport with the examiner and responded very well to any kind of praise or encouragement. He was even able to relate well to playful interaction between the examiner and himself. John was well dressed and seemed to be able to take care of his basic needs.

In terms of the activity level, John was able to sit on his chair for the first half-hour. After this time, an increasing level of activity was seen but the hyperactivity was always of manageable proportions. The examiner could see, however, how this hyperactivity could be a little bit of a problem in the classroom situation where he would have to spend more time and be more loosely supervised.

Test Results:

Bender Gestalt: Five figures were administered. With the possible exception of the circle, the figures lost their Gestalt so that they were completely unrecognizable. The quality of the drawings would place John at the bottom of the standardizing population.

Wechsler Intelligence Scale for Children, Revised Form (WISC-R)
(unstandardized Spanish translation used)
Full Scale IQ = 45 (Mentally Retarded Range)
Verbal Scale IQ = 45 (Mentally Regarded Range)

Information, scaled score	= 0
Comprehension	= 2
Arithmetic	= 0
Similarities	= 4
Digit Span	= (1)
Vocabulary	= 0

Performance Scale IQ = 46 (Mentally Retarded Range)

Coding	= 1
Picture Completion	= 3
Block Design	= 2
Picture Arrangement	= 2
Object Assembly	= 3

Discussion:

John is functioning at a very low, mentally retarded level. His highest score (Similarities) does not suggest the presence of any higher abilities since it is the result of his being able to answer only one test item correctly. There were, therefore, no indications in the tests administered of a higher capacity in any of the areas tested.

The test findings are supported by the child's history. The retardation of the language development was very extreme and goes along with a severe level of intellectual impairment. Moreover, the other problems, like the peculiar relationship with other children, may also be reflecting his low level of intellectual abilities.

Conclusion and Recommendations:

On the basis of the present evaluation, the examiner would suggest placing John in a lower-level EMH room. This placement may be too advanced for him on the basis of the IQ alone. John, however, has no physical disabilities, has mastered the hygiene and primary care training, and is able to communicate emotionally with others. If, after a period of time, it is felt that the material usually taught at this level is too complicated for John, a referral to a TMH room would then be appropriate.

The following specific recommendations may be considered once John has been placed:

1. Training in basic communication skills. Included here would be improving his vocabulary, learning the use of numbers, perhaps learning to form some sentences.
2. Training of "living skills" like the use of money, the recognition of coins of different denominations, the use of a clock and the concept of time, etc.
3. Help in social skills. As is often the case with individuals of his intellectual level, John tends to feel inadequate with other children and to be abused by them. Teaching of appropriate behaviors with other children would be very beneficial.
4. Helping the Fernandez family accept and adjust to John's limitations. Although the frustration and protectionism of Mrs. Fernandez is understandable, the father could be an ally in helping John to behave in the most appropriate manner that he is capable of.

Since children with intellectual impairments have neurological findings, and since John was the product of a possibly traumatic birth and has been on psychotropic medications in the past, the examiner would very strongly recommend a full neurological workup. At the very least a neurologist could evaluate the need for further medication. Ruling out the presence of an active and treatable neurological disorder seems also of primary importance.

In terms of long-term goals, the examiner would recommend that a psychological reevaluation is undertaken every few years in order to be able to assess any progress that is made. Good vocational training some time in the future would also seem of great importance.

III.E: NEUROPSYCHOLOGICAL TESTING

1. Neuropsychological testing is a method for diagnosing intellectual deficiencies that result from organic brain damage. It should be kept in mind that the relationship between neuropathology and intellectual impairment is not one-to-one. Many individuals who have a neurological disorder do not show any intellectual impairment and some intellectual deficits may be due to lack of innate ability. However, more often than not, substantial intellectual deficits in adults are due to neuropathology, so that it is possible to reach some conclusions about one, knowing the other.
2. A good way to organize the material in this area is to think of the brain as a refined computer. Three operations may be distinguished: the input, the process and the output. Figure 4 presents a chart that demonstrates this computer model of the brain.
3. The *Input* may be external or internal and includes a perception of the organism's own behaviors. The external input involves the stimulation of some receptor (e.g., the eye), the transmission of the stimulus through nerves, and the activation of the cells in some part of the cortex. The visual area is located in the occipital cortex, the auditory in the temporal lobe, and the tactile and kinesthetic in the post central gyrus. These cortical areas are organized in three levels. The primary level functions as a screen unto which the stimulus is projected. The secondary and tertiary levels function by grouping the stimuli in a way that

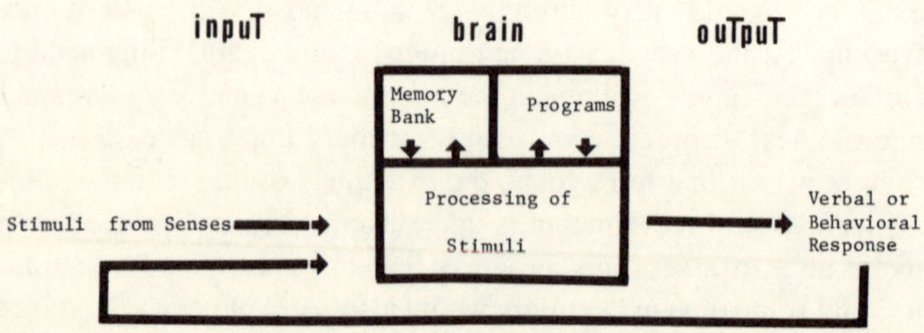

Figure 4. Chart Demonstrating a Computer Model of the Brain

TABLE 7: Main *Input* Functions of the Brain

FUNCTION		*POSSIBLE DISORDERS*	*BRAIN LOCATIONS*	*SUGGESTED METHOD OF EVALUATION*
Attention		Inability to concentrate on incoming stimuli	Hypocampus Amygdala	
SENSATION	Visual	Hemianopia: loss of sector of visual field	Occipital Lobe	Neurological Exam
		Scotomata: loss of isolated areas of visual field	Occipital Lobe	Neurological Exam
		Unilateral spatial agnosia: unawareness of one side of visual field	Contralateral Parieto-Temporal	Bender Gestalt
	Auditory	Reduction of auditory acuity	Lateral Temporal	Neurological Exam
	Tactile	Loss of sensation in some part of the body	Contralateral Post Central Gyrus	Neurological Exam
	Kinesthetic	Afferent paresis: inability to control gross movement due to lack of kinesthetic input	Contralateral Post Central Gyrus	Neurological Exam
		Afferent motor aphasia: difficulty in articulation (confusion of similar articulemes) due to lack of kinesthetic input	Dominant Post Central Gyrus	

TABLE 8: Main *Process* Functions of the Brain (D = dominant, ND = nondominant hemisphere)

	FUNCTION	*POSSIBLE DISORDERS*	*BRAIN LOCATIONS*	*SUGGESTED METHOD OF EVALUATION*
	PLANNING	Inability to function in a purposeful manner	Frontal Lobes	Wechsler's Picture Arrangement, Wechsler's Arithmetic, etc.
	TRACKING	Inability to shift attention from one incoming stimulus to another	Frontal Lobes	Wechsler's Digit Symbol, Trail Making Test
PERCEPTION	Visual	Optic Agnosia: inability to synthesize elements of objects into recognizable wholes	ND - Parieto-Occipital	Bender Gestalt; Hooper Visual Organization Test
		Simultaneous Agnosia: inability to perceive more than one object at a time	ND - Parieto-Occipital	
		Optic Alexia: inability to perceive letters as words	D - Parieto-Occipital	Aphasia Screening Test
		Inability to form visual image associated with word	D - Temporo-Occipital	Aphasia Screening Test
	Auditory	Acoustic Agnosia or Sensory Aphasia: inability to synthesize auditory stimuli into a recognizable whole (receptive language capacity)	D - Temporal	Aphasia Screening Test
		Sensory Amusia: inability to synthesize rhythms or sounds	ND - Temporal	Seashore Rhythm Test
	Tactile	Astereognosis: inability to synthesize tactile stimuli into a recognizable whole	D - Parietal	Rey's Skin Writing Test
	Kinesthetic	Disburbed Body Scheme or perception of body (usually leads to dressing apraxia or difficulty in dressing)	ND - Parietal	Neurological Exam

TABLE 8: Continued

FUNCTION	*POSSIBLE DISORDERS*	*BRAIN LOCATIONS*	*SUGGESTED METHOD OF EVALUATION*
Kinesthetic Perception, Continued	Afferent Apraxia: inability to synthesize kinesthetic input leading to disturbance of fine motor movement	Post Central Gyrus	Neurological Exam
	Anosognosia: inability to recognize own defects or errors	ND-Parietal	
MEMORY	Amnesic Aphasia: inability to recall names	D-Parietal D-Temporal	Aphasia Screening Test
	Optic Aphasia: inability to recall visual images in response to spoken words (i.e., draw figure of object named)	D-Temporo-Occipital	Aphasia Test
	Acoustic Amnesia: disturbance of audio-verbal memory	D-Temporal	Wechsler Memory Scale
	Disturbance of spatial memory	D-Parieto-Occipital	Wechsler Memory Scale Benton Visual Retention Test
COGNITION	Spatial disorientation: inability to find bearings in spatial coordinates	D-Parieto-Occipital	
	Construction Apraxia: inability to understand spatial designs	D-Parieto-Occipital	Wechsler's Block Design Wechsler's Object Assembly
	Inability to understand logical-grammatical relationships	D-Parieto-Occipital	Wechsler's Arithmetic Wechsler's Similarities

allows the organism to "synthesize" or "understand" them. For instance, stimulation of the primary visual cortex may lead to the perception of a flash of light; stimulation of the secondary zones may lead to the perception of images of objects or familiar persons that are seen in a moving, meaningful and dynamic way. Table 7 reviews the main input functions of the brain, diagnosable disorders involving those functions, the possible brain location of damaged tissue and some suggestions as to methods of evaluation.

4. The *Process* operation involves the following:
   a) A "plan of attack" which includes an understanding of what has to be accomplished and the organization of the organism towards the goal-directed behavior of accomplishing the given task.
   b) Search for the needed information. This function represents a control of the input activities by the process operation.
   c) Perception or interpretative integration of the Input.
   d) Memory or interpretative integration of the present input with past experiences.
   e) Cognition or the ability to go beyond the concrete input and make abstract interpretations.

   The frontal lobes play the very important function of organizing the person's behavior so that he performs in a goal-directed way. The rest of the process functions are carried on generally by the secondary and tertiary levels of the cortex. The mode specificity is still apparent so that, for instance, the formation of visual images associated with spoken words relies on the temporo-occipital cortex, integrating the verbal modality based on the temporal lobe with the visual modality of the occipital lobe. There is also a hemispheric specificity with a proneness for the dominant hemisphere to process the verbal and logical material. Table 8 reviews the information pertaining to the process operation of the brain.
5. Finally, the *Output* operation consists of movement which includes speech and relies on the frontal lobe's organizational capacity and the movement functions of the pre-central gyri. Further information is given in Table 9.
6. It should be obvious that one cannot test one operation in iso-

TABLE 9: Main *Output* Functions of the Brain (D = dominant, ND = nondominant hemisphere)

FUNCTION	*POSSIBLE DISORDERS*	*BRAIN LOCATIONS*	*SUGGESTED METHOD OF EVALUATION*
Movement	Inability to move in a smooth and integrated manner	ND-Precentral Gyrus	Neurological Exam Tapping Rhythms Finger Tapping Test
Speech	Efferent motor aphasia: inability to flow from one sound to the next (one single sound presents no problem regardless of sound)	D-Precentral	Aphasia Screening Test
	Word substitution with incorrect but better known words	Frontal Lobes	
	"Broca's Aphasia": difficulty in organizing words into meaningful speech	D-Frontal Lobe	

lation. Any task that the organism is asked to perform will involve some input, some processing and some output. A particular task, however, may involve a high level of difficulty in only one of the operations. For instance, the question, "How are an orange and a banana alike?" involves a relatively easy input and output and is, as a result, thought to test the thinking capacity of the organism. However, the diagnostician always has to keep in mind that, if the stimulus is not heard and perceived appropriately, the assumption that a particular question taps the thinking capacity may be erroneous.

7. A comprehensive neuropsychological evaluation involves testing the different parts of the system in an attempt to determine the nature of any deficiency. The basic premise is that any intellectual function can be impaired as the result of organic damage. Since the function of different parts of the brain are known, once the existence of a particular deficiency has been established, it is sometimes possible to pinpoint the location of the damage.
8. The comprehensive neuropsychological evaluation is probably best accomplished through the use of a test battery that systematically assesses the different functions. There are two well-known batteries in existence. The oldest of the two is the Halstead-Reitan Organic Battery. The newer Luria-Nebraska Neuropsychological Battery is much less expensive and has a well-explained theoretical basis, but is still experimental at this time. Most neuropsychologists, however, use a much reduced starting battery and go from there to test the specific functions involved in the presenting complaint. A common starting battery includes a Wechsler Intelligence Scale, the Bender Gestalt, the Wechsler Memory Scale and an Aphasia Evaluation.
9. The *Screening* approach is a less sophisticated way of evaluating individuals for possible neurological deficits. No one believes any longer in the assumption that all individuals with an Organic Brain Syndrome will respond in a similar way to psychological tests. It is now known that the functions impaired differ from one individual to another and are related to the location and the extent of the damaged tissue, as well as the length of time that has transpired since the damage took place. Nevertheless, it is

also true that some functions are more prone to be impaired in individuals who have an organic brain damage than others. This fact makes it possible to use, for screening purposes, an instrument that taps a very limited number of functions and can be administered in a very short period of time. There are several screening instruments on the market with differing degrees of complexity. Some of the single-task instruments are so effective, however, that their accuracy is not easily surpassed. Recommended instruments are:

a) The Category Test of the Reitan-Halstead Battery—shown to predict correctly 94% of the brain damaged, misdiagnosing only 6% of the normal subjects as brain damaged (Shaw, D. J. The reliability and validity of the Halstead Category Test. *Journal of Clinical Psychology,* 1966, 22, 176-79).
b) The Trail Making Test—shown to discriminate effectively between the normal population and the individuals known to have organic damage (Reitan, R. M. The validity of the Trail Making Test as an indicator of brain damage. *Perceptual and Motor Skills,* 1958, 8, 271-76).

It should be noted that screening instruments lose substantial efficiency when the task is to discriminate between organic and psychiatric patients.

10. The most defensible way of diagnosing organicity is by comparing premorbid and postmorbid test scores. Any significant drop of scores measuring a particular function beyond what is expected as a result of aging would be presumably due to an organic impairment. However, seldom does the examiner have the advantage of available premorbid scores. In most cases the examiner has to estimate the original level of ability. This estimate is made on the basis of the individual's median (and presumably unimpaired) scores and information obtainable from the client, like the amount of schooling completed. Low scores are then evaluated in the light of this estimate.
11. The diagnosis of neuropathology has been greatly improved with recent developments in neurology like the electroencephalogram and the computer-assisted brain scan techniques. As a result, the emphasis in neuropsychology is shifting from diagnosis to the ability to use the intellectual evaluation in order

to determine the areas of difficulty so that some remediation is possible. Rehabilitation of neurologically impaired subjects is clearly an area where psychologists can make a sizeable contribution. It is, however, a new field, without established training programs or bodies of knowledge.

12. The following books are recommended for further readings in the area of neuropsychological assessments:

    Gardner, E. *Fundamentals of Neurology: A Psychophysiological Approach*. Philadelphia: Saunders, 1975.

    Lezak M. D. *Neuropsychological Assessment,* New York: Oxford University Press, 1976.

    Luria, A. R. *The Working Brain: An Introduction to Neuropsychology*. New York: Basic Books, 1973.

Report Outline

1. The Referral Question:

a) Problems already noted.
b) Past injuries or medical problems that could result in an organic brain syndrome.
c) Rationale for further assessment or kind of information needed.

2. Behavioral Observations:

a) Appearance (can be omitted when the persons for whom the report is written know the client well or when the appearance is unremarkable).
b) Description of the quality of the examiner-patient interactions.
c) General behavior (personal comments made, unusual behavior, etc.).
d) Specific test behavior (motivation, defensiveness, attitude towards testing, etc.).

3. Test Results:

List the tests used and the scores obtained.

4. Discussion of Test Results:

a) A general statement giving the overall level of ability is usually followed by a discussion of the possibility of an OBS.

b) Two levels of conceptualization or distance away from actual scores may be possible:
   (1) One step removed from actual scores would be a conceptualization dealing with the specific abilities in which the client had difficulty. An example would be stating that a patient whose scores on the Wechsler Memory Scale and the Benton Visual Retention Test were depressed has a memory deficit.
   (2) Two steps away from the actual scores would be at the level of providing a neurological or etiological reason for the organic involvement. An example would be blaming an alcoholic deterioration in a patient who has drunk very heavily for years. For most psychologists this is outside of their area of expertise so that they have to be rather tentative and speculative when they make statements of this kind.

c) The question of how impaired the patient is as a result of an existing organic deficiency is also usually discussed.

5. *Recommendations:*

a) In cases where the deterioration is severe, the need for placement has to be addressed.
b) When the patient has not been seen by a neurologist and an organic involvement appears probable, a neurological workup should be recommended.
c) Finally, suggestions regarding how to deal with the patient in the light of the intellectual deficiency should be made.

Report Example

Name:	H.D.	*Age:* 54	*Race:* White
Address:	—— Hotel, Chicago, IL		
Marital Status:	Single	*Phone:* 649-3381	
Occupation:	Disabled Social Worker		

Reason for Request:

Mr. D. obtained a Bachelor degree from Harvard and was a social worker until very recently. After an argument with his supervisor, the patient quit his job and went to California without much of a plan. Upon his return to Chicago, he came to the Emergency Room stating that he hears knocks on the walls of his hotel room that do not allow him to sleep. Help is needed in differentiating diagnosis: Please rule out an Organic Brain Syndrome.

Tests Administered:

Bender Gestalt and Wechsler Adult Intelligence Scale.

Date of Administration:

October 29, 1974

Behavioral Observations:

Mr. D. accepted the testing and was very cooperative throughout the procedure. At times his hands were very tremulous and, although this continued throughout the testing, it seemed worst at the beginning. Mr. D. paid considerable attention to the instructions and put forth quite a bit of effort into the task, counting the dots that made up a figure and the like. The patient is right-handed but stated that he had been having some difficulty with his left hand, to the point that he had some trouble putting his arm into the coat sleeve.

Test Results:

Bender Gestalt, description of figures: Considerable difficulty is seen, especially in the more complex figures. In at least three of the figures, the gestalt is lost. There were some spacing problems so that one figure ran into the next.

Wechsler Adult Intelligence Scale:

Full Scale IQ = 97 (Normal Range)

Verbal Scale IQ = 107		Performance Scale IQ = 84	
Information, Scaled Score	= 13	Digit Symbol, scaled score	= 6
Comprehension	= 12	Picture Completion	= 8
Arithmetic	= 4	Block Design	= 2
Similarities	= 16	Picture Arrangement	= 7
Digit Span	= 2	Object Assembly	= 6
Vocabulary	= 18		

Trail Making Test:

Part A - 86 sec
Part B - 116 Sec

Discussion:

If Mr. D's intellectual ability is estimated on the basis of his good scores, it would be placed in the superior range and at the top of the standardizing population. This estimate is supported by the educational achievements that Mr. D. was capable of attaining in the past.

The present scores show a marked impairment of intellectual functioning. The verbal and concept formation areas appear to be fairly intact. In comparison, however, the patient is unable to keep track of more than one thing at a time as shown by his poor scores on Arithmetic, Digit Span and the Trail Making Test. He also has great difficulty with construction tasks (Bender, Block Design) and is probably showing an overall impairment of all performance tasks.

The functions that Mr. D. has trouble with are commonly impaired by the presence of an Organic Brain Syndrome. Given the scores and the existence of the motor problems noted above, the diagnosis of organicity can be made with a fair degree of confidence.

Recommendation:

A neurological evaluation is now recommended in order to try to determine the cause of the impairments.

III.F: TESTING FOR PSYCHODYNAMICS

1. In keeping with a systemic approach, when testing for psychodynamics the readers are encouraged to assess the following areas:
   a) The basic personality structure (see Section I.B and I.C for more information).
   b) The basic dynamic issues in the client's life (e.g., unresolved feelings left by the suicide of the client's father at an early age).
   c) Environmental factors that may be active at present and that are important in understanding the client's state of mind (often these factors are related to either 1a or 1b above).

   d) The pathology or inadaptive behaviors that the client presently demonstrates.
2. A systemic evaluation cannot be done well without a good knowledge of the patient's history. A "blind" interpretation of personality tests is an interesting academic exercise but makes much of the testing hard to interpret and precludes integration of information. In clinical situations, it needlessly places the examiner at a disadvantage. As a result, if a good history is not already available, the examiner is encouraged to do a thorough interview at the beginning of the evaluation (see Sections III.A and III.B for more details).
3. The emotional make-up of a person leaves an imprint on anything that the person does. The author, for instance, remembers obtaining a lot of useful data from watching a group of patients play a competitive table game. The information that follows, however, will be restricted to tests that were especially designed as psychodiagnostic tools.
4. Personality tests may be of two types:
   a) Personality inventories
   b) Projective techniques
5. Personality inventories are standardized questionnaires that the subject answers by himself. Table 10 gives information about the commonly used personality inventories. The better inventories were constructed through "empirical keying," a process that guarantees that the items included have diagnostic significance. These tests have the advantage of not taking much of the examiner's time, being able to be used by examiners with little training, and having relatively high validity and reliability. Their disadvantages are that, since they are much more structured than the projective techniques, the amount of information that they give is more limited; they tend to force the subjects into molds; they rely on the subjects' ability to perceive themselves accurately, and finally, they rely on the subjects' willingness to share their own self-images in a nondefensive manner.
6. Projective techniques, on the other hand, are fairly unstructured: the subject is encouraged to give some material that is later interpreted. Table 11 gives information about the projective techniques that are commonly used. Projective techniques require a

TABLE 10: Commonly Used Personality Inventories

Test Name	*Scoring*	*Major Areas Evaluated*	*Recommended References*
California Personality Inventory	Auto & Manual	480 items measuring poise, ascendency, self assurance, adequacy, socialization, responsibility, intrapersonal values, character, achievement potential, intellectual efficiency and interests	Megargee, E. I. *The California Psychological Inventory Handbook*. San Francisco: Jossey-Bass, 1972. Test manual
Edwards Personality Inventory	Auto & Manual	225 items measuring achievement, deference, order, exhibition, autonomy, affiliation, intraception, succorance, dominance, abasement, nurturance, change, endurance, heterosexuality and aggression	Test manual
Millon Multiaxial Clinical Inventory (MMCI)	Auto & Manual	775 items measuring the 8 personality styles (see Section I.B.) and anxiety, hysterical tendencies, hypomania, depression, alcohol and drug abuse, psychotic thinking, psychotic depression, delusions as well as schizoid, cycloid and paranoid tendencies	Test manual Millon, T. *Modern Psychopathology*. Philadelphia: Saunders, 1969
Minnesota Multi-Phasic Personality Inventory (MMPI).	Auto & Manual	566 items measuring validity of results and hypochondriasis, depression, hysterical tendencies, psychopathy, gender identity, paranoia, psychasthenia, schizophrenia, hypomania and social introversion. There is also a multitude of experimental scales.	Test manual Lachar, D. *The MMPI: Clinical Assessment and Automated Interpretation*. Los Angeles: Western Psychological Services, 1974 Graham, J. R. *The MMPI: A Practical Guide*. New York: Oxford University Press, 1977
Sixteen Personality Factors (16PF)	Manual	187 items measuring 16 interpersonal trait continuums like reserved vs. outgoing, practical vs. imaginative, dependent vs. self-sufficient, etc.	Test manual

TABLE 11: Commonly Used Projective Techniques

Name	*Major Areas Evaluated*	*Recommended References*
Draw-a-Person	View of self and members of opposite sex	
Family drawings	View of self and meaningful others	
Rorschach Ink-Blot Test	Personality style Dynamic issues Psychopathology	Beck, S. J., Beck, K., Levitt, E. and Molish, H. *Rorschach's Test,* New York: Grune and Stratton, 1961. Klopfer, B., Ainsworth, M., Klopfer, W. and Holt, R. *Rorschach Technique.* New York: Harcourt, Brace and World, 1954. Exner, J. F. *The Rorschach Systems.* New York: Grune and Stratton, 1969.
Thematic Apperception Test	Personality style Dynamic issues Interpersonal relations	Tomkins, S. S. *The Thematic Apperception Test.* New York: Grune and Stratton, 1947.

lot of training, take considerable time to administer, and interpretations are much more subjective than they are with the inventories. Nevertheless, in the hands of capable examiners, they can yield many useful insights about the subject.

Report Outline

1. The Referral Question:

a) Problems already noted

b) Rationale for further evaluation
c) Type of information that it would be helpful to obtain

2. Family History (often omitted):

a) Ethnic and socioeconomic status of family of origin
b) Brief description of members of the family
c) Brief description of the manner in which the patient related to the most significant members
d) Important events that took place in the family of origin
e) Description of the present family if it is not the family of origin
f) Description of the relationship between the patient and the present family members
g) Important events that have taken place in the present family

3. Educational and Vocational History (often omitted):

a) Extent of the education received
b) Motivation and ability of the patient as a student
c) Social relationships developed while going through school
d) Types and period of employment obtained
e) Success and satisfaction with job
f) Social interactions with co-workers

4. Behavioral Observations:

a) Appearance
b) Description of patient-examiner interactions
c) General behaviors (personal comments made by the patient, unusual behaviors, etc.)
d) Specific test behaviors (motivation, defensiveness, attitude towards testing, etc.)

5. Intellectual Assessment:

Some statement regarding the patient's general intellectual abilities should be made. When areas of intellectual strengths and weaknesses are known, they can also be made explicit. If an organic impairment is suspected, this issue should be discussed. Finally, personality aspects that affect the client's intellectual functioning (e.g., anxiety) can be discussed.

6. *Emotional Assessment:*

a) Basic personality structure—Habitual patterns, view of self and the world, usual way of relating to others.
b) Dynamic issues—Conscious and unconscious motivations.
c) Situational aspects—Situations where subject excels, situations that may present difficulties, present situation.
d) Pathology—Defenses or pathological reactions.

7. *Recommendations:*

Should include:
a) Suggestions of changes in the environment that would decrease the amount of stress.
b) Suggestions of changes in the psychic process that would make the individual better able to cope with the world.
c) Concrete ways of achieving these changes.

Should avoid inappropriateness:
a) No recommendation should be made when the purpose of the evaluation was simply to gain more information.
b) No recommendation should be made in areas where the examiner is not qualified (e.g., type of medication).
c) It is often felt that no recommendation should be made in an area where the professional receiving the report is obviously qualified to arrive at his or her own conclusions.

8. *Summary*

Report Example

Name: Jane Peters
Address: 127 Main, Chicago, IL
Age: 18
Referred by: Dr. M.

Referral Problem:

Jane is complaining of headaches which she has had off and on since high school. She feels that the frequency of the headaches has increased recently. This latter development coincided with a time in which she was having some difficulties in a small college where she was studying to become a teacher. She eventually quit this school planning to take a course by correspondence and transfer to a school that would be more to her liking. The increased headaches, however, have made it impossible for her to follow her plans at this time. The present evaluation was undertaken in an effort to understand the dynamics of the patient's problems.

Family History:

The patient's father, Mr. Peters, is a 45-year-old carpenter who works for a nearby hospital. He seemed somewhat concerned about his daughter and drove her on every occasion to the examiner's office for her appointment. When asked to describe her father, Jane had some difficulty but eventually said that he was "ambitious, hard-working, and liked to keep busy." Jane also had the same difficulty with her mother whom she simply described as "ambitious too." The mother is 44 years old and works as a part-time clerk. As long as Jane can remember, her mother has suffered from "migraine headaches." Her mother's headaches, however, are apparently less frequent than the patient's and are well-controlled with medication.

There are two children in the Peters family. Jane is presently 18 and her sister is four years younger. Jane's sister is a freshman in high school and is described as "stubborn and having a lot of determination." Although they have had their fights, Jane feels that generally they get along well.

Educational and Vocational History:

Jane went to a small elementary school of a religious denomination. She obtained acceptable grades and enjoyed this experience. When she graduated, she went to a large public high school that she did not like. Her distaste for this school was blamed on its size and the fact that a person could never feel the security of knowing everyone around. She started dating a few years ago and states that there is no problem in this area. She, however, plans not to get married in the near future and does not date in a serious manner.

Last September, Jane entered a small college where she was hoping to become a teacher. She had demonstrated an interest in this area for some time and had gained some experience by volunteering as a teacher's aide. As already noted, at this time she has quit this school and plans to continue in another.

Jane states that her parents exert no pressure with regard to the vocational choice. The impression was, nevertheless, that she sees them as "ambitious" people who have some expectations for her.

Behavioral Observations:

Jane was always on time and very neatly dressed. Her clothes were of a style that made her look older than she really is. She talked readily and often had numerous questions about the testing procedure before the testing took place. Also, she frequently made comments with regard to the examiner's behavior. She observed, for instance, how the examiner was always writing and how the examiner avoided answering questions regarding the interpretation of a particular test item, traits that she felt the examiner had in common with Dr. M.

Jane informed the examiner that he and Dr. M. had only a few weeks to make her headaches go away. If in a few weeks the situation had not improved, she was planning to move on to another doctor. This comment led to a brief discussion about therapy and its purpose and methods. Jane listened to the comments made and seemed able to accept them.

The patient appeared interested and motivated for testing. She gave no indication of any difficulty understanding the instructions. With the Rorschach and the T.A.T., however, she was a little resistant and made attempts to put them down as "stupid" or "unproductive."

Intellectual Evaluation:

The Bender Gestalt shows well-drawn figures that are fairly well spaced. The lines of the last figure are not totally straight but no other difficulties are apparent. The Wechsler Adult Intelligence Scale shows the following scores:

Full Scale IQ = 98 (Normal Range)

Verbal Scale IQ = 98		Performance Scale IQ = 98	
Information	= 8	Picture Completion	= 9
Comprehension	= 10	Block Design	= 9
Arithmetic	= 9	Picture Arrangement	= 9
Similarities	= 12	Object Assembly	= 11
Digit Span	= 7		
Vocabulary	= 9		

All of Jane's scores are in keeping with an average level of intellectual ability. There are no major deviations except, perhaps, for Digit Span, which probably indicates the presence of anxiety. The scores give no evidence of intellectual or memory impairment.

Emotional Evaluation:

Jane has a fairly strong tendency towards an obsessive-compulsive personality style. One of the most pronounced aspects of this tendency was Jane's fear of disclosure. Her conservative dress style and the manner of questioning the examiner before giving any information were already noted. Furthermore, in both the Rorschach and the T.A.T., she responded as little and as unrevealingly as possible. In the Rorschach, for instance, she only gave eight responses. She behaves as if she felt that openness could only make her vulnerable and therefore should be avoided.

A second aspect in the obsessive-compulsive personality is the issue of control. Her control over the environment could be seen in the way she structured the interviews with her questions. Telling the examiner that he only had a brief period of time to accomplish results was another way of letting the examiner know who was at the helm. Her control over her emotions is also apparent. Her Rorschach was void of color responses; her T.A.T. stories were overly factual and seldom considered any feelings. Not infrequently, her inner control is at the expense of her honesty with herself. On card 17 of the T.A.T., for instance, she told the following story:

> This is taking place over in France. The girl on the bridge is looking over and watching the fish below. She is wishing how she would like to be a fish. But . . . she knows that she can't be a fish because she doesn't even know how to swim. Anyway, she is really satisfied with her life the way it is.

In this story the wish-fulfilling fantasy of becoming a fish is rejected, rationalized and suppressed.

Jane's tendency towards accuracy and perfectionism is yet another aspect of her obsessive-compulsiveness. In the Rorschach she objected, for instance, to several of the blots as being "messy" or not allowing any possible response. It seemed as if she would reject anything that was not exactly right. The T.A.T. stressed the need for the characters to do the right thing as well as the happy endings that follow when the right action is taken.

Finally, guilt usually has an important role in individuals with obsessive-compulsive tendencies. The strength that guilt can have in Jane's life is shown by her story to card 13 of the T.A.T.:

> The man in the picture has just killed his wife. He makes the room look like it was a robbery and someone else killed her. The police agree with this and the man is found innocent. But, due to his conscience, he tries to sleep at night but can't. So, after six months, he confesses to the murder. He is then put in jail for 10 or 15 years.

People who have this type of personality have some definite advantages. They tend to be moral, productive and law-abiding citizens. They are hard-working individuals who perform well in jobs that call for accuracy. They are punctual and responsible. The price they pay can be seen in the aspects that have already been discussed.

There are times when a person with obsessive-compulsive tendencies may be expected to experience more difficulties in life. It can be argued, for instance, that late adolescence and young adulthood may be very taxing. It is a period when the "right" path ceases to be clear. Where often before, individuals only had to do as they were told, now they are expected to gain some independence and to act on their own. Also, it is a period when expectations may test the limits of a person's abilities. The latter issue seems to be more of a preoccupation for Jane. The issue of expectations appears on several T.A.T. stories. Card 6, for instance, portrays a man and a woman in the midst of a discussion. According to Jane they are discussing their "stepson" and "whether or not he should go on to become a doctor or take over his father's business." Although the parents feel that this is too much, the son decides to do both, work for his father part-time and go to medical school. The story demonstrates the unrealistically high goals that Jane holds for herself.

On a card where wish-fulfilling fantasies are often given, Jane tells the following story:

> There is a girl on the picture who is horseback riding along

> the lakefront, something she does every morning as the sun rises. She then goes into her mansion and changes clothes, getting into a swimsuit. She goes into her backyard, into the heated pool and practices her swimming because she is a professional swimmer. The maid makes a dinner and all is ready for when her husband comes home. The husband is an executive in a big firm. After dinner they get into a plane to California because she has a swim meet in two days. Her husband goes with her because he is behind her, backing her up. She wins the swim meet and they fly back home.

The story epitomizes all the points that have already been discussed: the need for support from others, together with the need to be someone in her own right; the obsessive-compulsive outlook on the world (the daily routine, the belief that success will always follow those that behave in the right manner, etc.); and finally, the grandiose expectations for herself.

Jane's headaches make sense from a psychological point of view. On the one hand, they are the tense response of her organism to unachievable expectations. On the other hand, they have important secondary benefits since they take her out of the competition and give her an excuse for her failures.

Recommendations:

It would seem that at a time when the environment is taxing Jane's power to cope with it, making her comfortable in the therapeutic situation would be a good goal. In order to make her comfortable, the therapist could go along with her obsessive-compulsive tendencies. In keeping with this approach, the therapist would allow Jane as much control as possible of the situation. He may also make it very clear what Jane must do in order to fulfill her part of the contract and what she could hope to obtain in return.

A therapeutic exploration of Jane's present goals may be very beneficial. This exploration may be done with the therapist taking a very supportive role. With the support, she may be able to accept the unreality of her unconscious expectations without feeling like a failure. The goal would be to have Jane see herself as a good person who, for neurotic reasons, wanted to become a superhuman.

If this exploration is effective, with the realistic expectations we should see a lowering of the psychic tension and the disappearance of the symptomatology.

A different strategy would be to attempt to change, at least to some degree, the present personality structure. This goal would involve a more psychodynamic approach where the therapist would play a less supportive role. It would also demand much more motivation from Jane and more extensive financial and time commitments. However, reducing the level of her obsessive-compulsive tendencies and developing a more flexible and adaptive personality structure would have great benefits for years to come.

III.G: VOCATIONAL TESTING

1. In order to counsel an individual with regard to occupational choice, the following factors have to be considered:
   a) Abilities
   b) Achievement Motivation
   c) Personality Style
   d) Field of Interest
   e) Income and Employability Requirements
2. The level of intellectual ability can be evaluated through an IQ test. When specific areas are being considered, more specialized tests (for instance, a test of manual dexterity or tests of mechanical abilities) can be used to determine the individual's capacity.
3. The emotional ability to go through training is usually evaluated on the basis of past history and present level of pathology. The client is usually interviewed for this material, although personality tests can also be used.
4. The client's motivation is also assessed in a clinical manner by taking into account verbalizations with regards to training as well as past efforts.
5. The client's personality style can be done through a personality trait inventory (see recommendation under emotional evaluation).
6. Table 12 gives the relevant information concerning the vocational inventories that are commonly used.
7. Finally, the client's expectations regarding income and availa-

TABLE 12: Commonly Used Vocational Inventories

Test Name	*Scoring*	*Major Areas Evaluated*	*Recommended References*
Carreer Assessment Assessment Inventory (CAI)	Auto	305-item questionnaire measuring three types of scales: a) Occupational Theme Scales (6) describing the individual's overall work orientation, b) Basic Interest Scales (22) providing a measure of specific interests, and c) Occupational Scales (89) which relate to individual's interests to those of persons in the different carreers.	Test Manual
Kuder Preference Record	Manual	498 items that rate the individual's preferences on 9 occupational areas: mechanical, computational, scientific, persuasive, artistic, literary, musical, social service and clerical.	Test Manual
Strong-Campbell Interest Inventory (SCII)	Auto	325-item revision of the Strong Vocational Interest Blank. Recommended for individuals interested in carreers that require advance training. The test measures three types of scales as described above: a) General Occupational Themes (6), b) Basic Interest Scales (23) and c) Occupational Scales (124).	Test Manual

bility of work also have to be taken into consideration and discussed.

Report Outline

1. Reason for Referral:

The reason why it is felt that the person needs a vocational evaluation.

2. Educational History:

a) Amount of education completed
b) Degree of past academic success
c) Attitudes of the patient towards further education or training

3. Occupational History:

Jobs that the client has held in the past together with the period of time during which the client held the job and the objective and subjective success attained.

4. Behavioral Observations:

a) Appearance
b) Description of the quality of the examiner-client interactions
c) General behaviors (personal comments made, unusual behaviors, etc.)
d) Specific test behaviors (motivation, defensiveness, attitude towards testing, etc.)

5. Test Results:

Whenever possible, list the actual scores.

6. Discussion:

a) General level of abilities
b) Abilities that differ from this general level (weaknesses and strengths)
c) Personality style
d) Fields of interest
e) Amount of motivation
f) Discussion of occupations that fit enough of the issues addressed above to be good alternatives for this patient

7. Recommendations:

What the patient should do in the light of all the information given above, in order to improve vocational adjustment or opportunity.

Report Example

Reason for Request:

Mr. G is a 46-year-old white male who seems capable but has been unemployed for the past nine years. The patient carries a diagnosis of schizophrenia, chronic undifferentiated. At this time, he expresses a wish to receive vocational rehabilitation. Please evaluate.

Educational History:

Mr. G. was raised in the Chicago area where he went to a Catholic elementary school until he finished the primary grades. He recalls having no difficulties and always passing to the next grade at the end of the year. However, he was not a very good student nor was he particularly interested in academic matters. The patient continued his education by attending a public high school. He was then most interested in the science courses, although he tended to do poorly as far as final grades are concerned. Mr. G. failed some courses and had some trouble studying the material during the high school years, but he nevertheless managed to graduate. Since that time he has never involved himself in any kind of training or education.

Occupational History:

After his high school graduation Mr. G. did not have a clear idea of what he wanted to do with his life. He did want to leave his family of origin and felt that enlisting in the military service would be a practical way of accomplishing this end. During the four years that followed, the patient served in different locations in the United States without any difficulties. He did not particularly like some of the limitations that the military forced on him but was fairly well adjusted and productive during this time. Upon discharge, he was able to obtain a job as a bank teller which he held for a period of ten years. At first, he was able to perform his duties well and was reasonably happy with the job. During the last few years, however, he had become very discontented with the job, did not feel supported and appreciated by his superiors, and his emotional problems became increasingly more intrusive. Nine years ago he was given a sick leave while he was in the hospital and, when he ran out of sick leave, his employment was terminated. At the time Mr. G. felt relieved by the firing and has never attempted to get back into a regular job in any serious manner ever since.

Tests Administered:

Millon Multiaxial Clinical Inventory
Rorschach
Wechsler Adult Intelligence Scale
Strong Vocational
Kuder Preference

Dates of Administration:

September 19, 21, 23, 26, 1977

Behavioral Observations:

Mr. G was very interested in being examined and was cooperative throughout the four test sessions. With each succeeding examination period, Mr. G became less anxious, showing greater temerity, less hesitancy, more direct statements, fewer questions, and a more casual, unguarded conversation with the examiner.

Initially, the patient sought out the examiner to protest the difficulty of the Strong Inventory and required encouragement to continue. During the WAIS administration, Mr. G was only intermittently anxious—shaking his legs, rapidly smoking cigarettes and clicking his tongue against his teeth. Yet when he engaged in a personally meaningful task, like the arithmetic subtest, his anxious behavior markedly subsided or stopped. By the time the Rorschach was administered, Mr. G. was casually smoking cigarettes.

Intellectual Evaluation: Test Results:

Wechsler Adult Intelligence Scale:
Full Scale IQ = 92 (Normal Range)

Verbal Scale IQ = 95
Performance Scale IQ = 89

Information, scaled score	= 8	Digit Symbol, scaled score	= 8
Comprehension	= 9	Picture Completion	= 9
Arithmetic	= 12	Block Design	= 6
Similarities	= 10	Picture Arrangement	= 9
Digit Span	= 6	Object Assembly	= 6
Vocabulary	= 9		

Discussion of Intellectual Evaluation:

The WAIS Full Scale score indicates that Mr. G is functioning at the lower end of the normal range of intelligence. Despite the pressure of some test anxiety, this score is a representative measure of his current capabilities.

Personality Evaluation:

Mr. G's obsessive-compulsive nature permeates all of the testing results. Its effect can also be seen in the three main areas of emotional functioning—the cognitive area, the inner emotional (intrapersonal) area, and the interpersonal area.

From a cognitive point of view, Mr. G's perceptions tend to center on the small aspects of reality. This is shown in the Rorschach by the overuse of the small and unusual details. The patient's perceptions also tend to be rigid and concrete. Again, in the Rorschach, there is a tendency to base most of his responses on the form of the blot only, without taking into account the more intangible aspects of the stimuli. His obsessive tendency is particularly obvious in the WAIS where his highest score was on arithmetic, a subtest where orderliness and meticulousness pay off.

In their personal habits, obsessive-compulsive individuals tend to be efficient, dependable, industrious and persistent. Often they believe in discipline and practice self-restraint in a perfectionistic fashion.

The compulsive behavior style colors the way that Mr. G relates to others. The number of human responses that he gave on the Rorschach, for instance, was minimal, suggesting that the patient does not relate often to people. Since the obsessive-compulsive tendency is often seen as a manuever to gain distance from others, the finding fits in well. The findings also make sense because people tend to be less reliable than nonhumans and obsessive-compulsives look for situations that are structured in such a way that they can always predict the outcome.

Based on Mr. G's personality style we can also speculate that, when he does relate to others, he will tend to relate in a submissive manner with those who have a higher status and in a dominant manner with those of lower status. Finally, it can also be speculated that he will have some definite expectancies with regards to the roles that others will play in relationships with him.

It should be noted that when we refer to Mr. G as having an obsessive-compulsive personality style, the label is not used as a type of pathology. The label is used here merely for describing a flavor of his particular personality that involves the traits discussed above. The use of this label does not mean to imply the presence of a neurosis or of a character disorder.

In any event, given this personality style, it is not hard to understand the type of situation that has gotten Mr. G into trouble in the past. Problematic situations have been of two types: the first type is the situation in which Mr. G has a particular expectancy from others that is not fulfilled. For instance, on several occasions, Mr. G has demanded a specific action from "therapists." When his demands are not met, the patient becomes very disturbed. As discussed above, the obsessive-compulsive tends to have a well-conceptualized set of expectations. When others do not behave as expected, the basic premise of order and predictability is undermined, and this experience is perceived as upsetting.

The second problematic situation has been the scheduling and ordering of the patient's time in a meaningful manner. Mr. G finds himself with a lot of free time due to his prolonged disability. The lack of a meaningful schedule and a productive life is especially troublesome with a person who has rigid obsessive and perfectionistic goals.

Often the patient's coping mechanism breaks down when he is faced with one of the problem situations. His behavior is then marked with restlessness and agitation. His anxiety is seen behaviorally in the testing sessions through his constant leg movement. The lowest score of the WAIS was Digit Span, a subtest that is very sensitive to anxiety and the consequent lack of ability to concentrate. The

Rorschach shows the anxiety as well as some potential for acting out.

Vocational Evaluation:

Test Results: The Strong Vocational Inventory showed that Mr. G. is high on the "Conventional Theme." (Score = 60)
Subjects that score high on this theme:

> "Prefer jobs where they know exactly what they are supposed to do, using both verbal and numerical skills. They prefer office work but do not like to be leaders. They want to know exactly what is expected of them and generally prefer jobs that involve doing the same task over and over. They describe themselves as well controlled, reliable and stable. People on the following occupations have high scores on this theme: Bank clerks, statisticians, financial analysts, accountants, office managers and bookkeepers."

On the Special Interest Scale of the Strong, the patient scored highest on adventurous occupations. This finding is hard to interpret because it does not fit in at all with the rest of the information about the patient.

On the Strong Occupational Scales, Mr. G scored high on "printer, math or science teacher, senior CPA, pharmacist or computer programmer."

Finally, the Kuder Preference Record showed high scores on the clerical computational scales.

Discussion: On the Positive side, the interests shown on the Strong and Kuder inventories go along very well with the evaluation of the patient's ability and personality. His intellectual capacity is sufficient to warrant some sort of clerical training. The patient's obsessive-compulsive personality style would be an asset in the type of job where orderliness, meticulousness and dependability are important. A negative consideration, however, is that the patient has been unemployed for a fairly long period of time and—in spite of persistent psychotherapy—has not been able to control adequately the periods of agitation.

Recommendations:

Rather than continuing the unsuccessful attempts at "insight" therapy, the present writer would suggest a vocational rehabilitation plan. It is felt that the plan of most benefit to the patient would be training that would make him able to function as a clerk of some sort. This represents a good fit of the patient's interests, goals and intellectual abilities and should be tried first.

In the event that the patient's emotional instability makes him unable to receive the training necessary, the present writer feels that the patient should be helped to obtain a job at a maintenance or janitorial level. Although this will be less to the patient's liking, it would still provide some structure and fulfillment for Mr. G.

Neither one of the above goals can be accomplished without an ongoing and involved supportive psychotherapy program. The patient needs to feel all the time that there is an understanding and protective therapist whom he can depend on.

IV Patient Management

IV.A: THE PROBLEM-ORIENTED APPROACH

1. After the basic information about a patient has been gathered, the therapist needs to organize it in a comprehensive manner. This is best accomplished through the use of the Problem-Oriented Approach. This approach was first suggested by Hayes-Roth* and is now widely used.
2. Problem-oriented patient management calls for the following sequence:
   a) Construction of a problem list.
   b) Development of a treatment plan for each problem on the list.
   c) Negotiation of the treatment plans with client so that a treatment contract is established through which all participants agree on the plan of action.
   d) Fulfillment of the treatment contract.
3. The problem list should have all the concrete issues that are presented by the individual that may be considered "problems." Although it is impossible to present an exhaustive list, the author has compiled a list that provides fairly good coverage of the psychological areas of functioning. This list follows below.

Problem List

Somatic Functions

1. Psychomotor acceleration
   Overtalkativeness

*Hayes-Roth, F., Longabaugh, R. and Ryback, R. The problem-oriented medical record and psychiatry. *British Journal of Psychiatry*, 1972, 121, 27-34.

Decreased need for sleep

2. Psychomotor retardation
   Loss of energy
   Loss of motivation
3. Loss of appetite
4. Overeating
5. Insomnia
6. Excessive sleeping
7. Stomach or intestinal trouble
   Ulcers
   Headache
   Asthma
   Dizzy spells
   Other somatic complaints
   Preoccupation with somatic complaints
8. Medical illness or disability
9. Alcohol or drug abuse
10. Alcohol or drug intoxication

Intellectual Functions

11. Intellectual deficiency
12. Memory deficiency
13. Language deficiency
14. Inability to concentrate
    Short attention span
15. Confusion
    Incoherence
    Disorientation
16. Lack of ability to perceive or express emotion
17. Inability to make decisions
18. Tangentiality
    Flight of ideas
    Circumstantiality
    Irrelevancy
    Preoccupations
    Obsessions

Intrapsychic Functions

19. Inappropriate emotional response
20. Fluctuations of mood
    Irritability
    Explosiveness
21. Sadness
    Guilt
    Feelings of unworthiness
    Feelings of hopelessness
22. Suicidal feelings
23. Elation
    Overconfidence
    Feelings of omnipotence
24. Lack of confidence
    Feelings of inferiority
25. Bizarreness
    Awkwardness
26. Untidiness
    Bad personal hygiene
27. Impulsiveness
28. Irresponsible Behavior
29. Excessive need for attention
30. Tactlessness
31. Fears
    Phobias
    Anxiety, tension, agitation, restlessness
32. Feelings of depersonalization
    Feelings of unreality
    Unusual illusions or feelings
33. Rigidity
    Coldness or aloofness
    Emotional constriction
34. Denial
    Inability to accept an aspect of reality
35. Delusions
    Hallucinations

Social Functions

36. Lack of friends
    Loneliness
    Withdrawal
37. Shyness
    Discomfort in relating to others
    Fear of rejection
38. Overdependence, oversubmissiveness
39. Argumentativeness
    Obstructionism
40. Hostility
41. Homicidal feelings
42. Antisocial behavior
    Tendency to take advantage of others
43. Loss of meaningful other
44. Grandiosity
    Arrogance
45. Mistrust
    Suspiciousness
    Paranoid feelings
46. Tendency to dominate or overcontrol others

Family Functions

47. Irritation with behaviors of other family members
48. Argumentativeness
    Struggle for control
    Conflictual family system
49. Deficient communication in the family
50. Lack of differentiation of family members
    United front family system
51. Irresponsible behavior by family member
52. Rejection of family member
    Scapegoating
53. Interference by relatives
54. Lack of participation in family decisions
    Overadequate-underadequate family system

55. Inadequate parenting
56. Lack of stability of family relationships
    Lack of strength
57. Launching difficulties
    Inability of grown children to move out

Sexual Functions

58. Discomfort over homosexual tendencies
59. Wish to be of opposite sex
    Discomfort with sex-appropriate roles
60. Sexual overinhibition
61. Inability to get sexually aroused
62. Sexual promiscuity
63. Impotence
    Frigidity
    Repulsion by sexual thoughts
    Complaint of pain during sex
64. Inability to find sexual partner
65. Rejection by sexual partner
66. Attraction towards tabooed partner or abnormal object
67. Lack of information about sex
    Lack of sexual sophistication
68. Sexual incompatibility
69. Moral or legal problem results from individual's sexual behavior

Occupational Functions

66. Confusion over vocational or occupational goals
67. Unemployment
    Lack of school
68. Dissatisfaction with job or school

IV.B: DEVELOPING A TREATMENT PLAN

1. As discussed in Section II.B, emotional difficulties are the result of friction between the individual and the environment. A treat-

ment plan consists of measures that are proposed as a way of reducing this friction.

2. Possible attempts to reduce friction may involve changes in any one of the following spheres:
   a) The environment
   b) The organic make-up of the patient
   c) The patient's cognition
   d) The patient's affective response
   e) The patient's skills
   f) The therapeutic support
3. There are several ways in which changes to the *environment* may be attempted. They include:
   a) Changing the environment all together by moving the client to a different place of residence.
   b) Working to increase the tolerance of the environment for the problem that the patient presents.
   c) Working towards decreasing aspects of the environment that are considered to be causing or contributing to the problem or increasing aspects of the environment that are considered therapeutic.
   d) Having the environment give appropriate reinforcements and recognitions for the patient's behavior.
   e) Use hypnotic suggestions as a means through which a member of the environment (the therapist) can influence the patient's behavior.
4. In reference to the *organic make-up* of the patient, interventions may have any of the following goals:
   a) Evaluate and treat a physical disorder that is considered causative or contributory to the problem in question.
   b) Give the patient some medical treatment that changes his or her reactions to the environment. This medical treatment usually consists of either psychotropic medications (see Section V.E) or electric-shock treatment.
5. Changes in the patient's *cognitive system* are done with the hope that a change in the way that the patient views him or herself and the world will lead to changes in the way that patient feels about him or herself and the world as well as changes in his or her behavior. Furthermore, some cognitive changes are good

in their own right even if they do not lead to any other change. In any event, the interventions that can be made in this area include:

a) Increasing the patient's own awareness with respect to the problem.
b) Adding information that the patient needs or correcting some misinformation that the patient has.
c) Discovering and understanding secondary benefits that the patient obtains.
d) Increasing the conscious motivation that the client has to work on the problem by exploring with him or her the negative consequences that the problem has in his or her life.
e) Exploring if there are any specific situations in the patient's life that are prone to evoking or exacerbating the problem.
f) Exploring the historical dynamics or childhood origins of the problem.

6. The *affective response* refers to the feelings that the patient has about him or herself or the world. Any changes that are made to the individual or the environment may end up changing the affective response. However, some attempts are sometimes made to alter the emotional responses directly. These attempts include:
   a) Externalization of emotion with the goal of venting feelings that are overcontrolled or establishing contact with feelings that have been repressed.
   b) Working through of emotional material, a process that changes feelings through continued exposure and assimilation of situations similar to the situation that originally evoked the feelings in question.
7. Therapeutic training to improve the patient's *skills* can be:
   a) Corrective training which may involve giving the patient a skill that s/he did not have or changing the pattern of behavior that is evoked in the patient by a particular situation.
   b) Compensatory training which involves developing skills to cope with the problem rather than to solve it.
8. The area of *therapeutic support* deals with the kind of relationship that is established with the patient. The therapeutic support may be:

a) Ego-syntonic, as when the therapist establishes a relationship that is complementary to the client's personality make-up (see Section V.A for more information).
b) Problematic, as when the therapist establishes a relationship through which the patient is helped to solve some of his or her problems in living.

9. Table 13 gives a summary of the curative factors discussed above.
10. Given all the possible options, a therapist may decide to concentrate all efforts on one singular plan or to attempt to integrate several plans. It should be noted that, although it is possible to integrate many of the plans, some plans actually work in opposite directions from one another. For instance, the plan of establishing a supportive relationship that is in keeping with the client's personality style is hard to integrate with the plan of using corrective training in order to change that personality

TABLE 13: Summary of the Possible Therapeutic Plans.

1. Change of Environment
2. Increasing Environmental Tolerance
3. Environmental Reinforcements
4. Positive Environmental Changes
5. Hypnotic Suggestions

6. Treatment of Physical Disease
7. Psychotropic Medications

8. Increasing Awareness
9. Offering Information
10. Exploration of Secondary Benefits
11. Exploration of Negative Consequences
12. Exploration of Current Dynamics
13. Exploration of Historical Dynamics

14. Externalization of Emotion
15. Working Through

16. Corrective Training
17. Compensatory Training

18. Ego-syntonic Support
19. Problematic Support

style. The choice of curative plans that the therapist makes has to take three factors into consideration:

a) the ability of the patient to change,
b) the theoretical orientation and training of the therapist, and
c) the financial or practical considerations involved.

11. When considering the patient's ability to change, four factors should be taken into account:
    a) The patient's intellectual abilities (patients who are very dull or have an organic brain deficit tend to have low ability to change).
    b) The patient's motivation (low motivation is a bad prognostic indication for change).
    c) The level of pathology. As a rule, the more disturbed the patient is, the less able s/he will be to change. However, a lack of distress is also a bad prognostic indicator because it is then thought that the patient is "not hurting enough." It should be noted that the level of pathology may change while the patient is under treatment. When this happens, the evaluation of the patient's ability to change has to be reconsidered.
    d) The amount of social and family support that the patient has.

    The lower the estimate of the patient's ability to change, the more reliance has to be placed on environmental or organic changes. As the ability to change increases, the treatment plans can shift into cognitive, affective or training changes.
12. Schools of therapy often tend to emphasize one therapeutic plan more than others. The system presented here can be used by students from different orientations. It allows integration of the different orientations in a manner similar to that proposed by Arnold A. Lazarus in his book *Multimodal Behavior Therapy* (New York: Springer Publishing Company, 1976). Although this book is highly recommended, it unfortunately disregards the contribution of environmental changes and of the psychoanalytic approach.
13. Finally, because different levels demand different amounts of time and degrees of involvement from the therapist, the practical issues of available resources also has to be taken into consideration in developing a treatment plan.

IV.C: THE TREATMENT CONTRACT

1. The treatment contract involves a process by which both the patient and the therapist discuss the current problems of the patient and reach some sort of understanding regarding the goals and method of therapy.
2. The treatment contract has a particular chronological place in the management of a patient. It should take place after the basic information has been gathered and before therapeutic efforts are made. Although it usually stays fairly constant, it should be flexible enough so that significant new developments can lead to renegotiation of the contract.
3. Some therapists emphasize the importance of the contract by having a contract that:
   a) Is a written document which is kept by both patient and therapist (or treatment staff).
   b) States concretely and specifically what each individual is agreeing to do.
   c) Has stipulations of measurable changes that would be taken as indications that the problem is improved or solved.
4. Although most therapists today do not insist on such intricate contracts, no one denies the importance of reaching a clear understanding with the patient regarding acceptable plans and expectations.
5. In order to expedite this understanding the therapist should:
   a) Set an atmosphere in the treatment sessions which will be conducive to this type of negotiation (see Section IV.D for details).
   b) Bring the topic up for discussion when further discussion is needed.

IV.D: THERAPEUTIC BEHAVIORS

1. Therapists may be defined as individuals who have been trained to use themselves and their relationships with patients so as to help patients solve emotional difficulties in their lives.
2. From the above definition, it would follow that some behavioral

characteristics are generally important in the making of therapists. For instance:

a) Therapists should be flexible individuals who do not have to act in a particular way because of personal needs but who can behave in whatever way may be thought to help patients the most.
b) Therapists should be "professionals." They should be able to present themselves as individuals who are well trained for their particular job (or who are supervised by someone who is) and who would not take a case in which they could not do an adequate job. They should not be unduly nervous or fearful and should have some assurance in their ability to deal with treatment situations.
c) Therapists should have a certain degree of empathy. They should be able to understand how patients experience the world, to have some sympathy for their problems and to be interested in helping patients solve them.
d) Therapists should be "genuine." They should be aware and accepting of their own feelings. This does not mean that therapists have to be an "open book." They can, indeed, choose which feelings would be productive to share with patients and which would not be. What it does mean is that whatever part of the therapist the patient sees is real and not phony or put-on.
e) Therapists should have positive regard for patients. They should be able to accept patients at whatever level of functioning they are, without feeling that the patients are worthless or beyond help.
f) Therapists should be realistic, able to work with the patients' goals while accepting the constraints that are placed by the patients' abilities and the environment.
g) Therapists' behaviors should be always ethical and moral.

A discussion of some of these characteristics can be found in:

Rogers, C. R., *On Becoming a Person.* Boston: Houghton Mifflin, 1967.

3. There are also some behavioral characteristics that would be important for therapists to have in specific situations. Three such situations will be discussed: the diagnostic situation, the therapy

contract situation and the treatment situation.

4. The diagnostic situation usually calls for a passive stance on the part of therapists. The professionals in this situation are mainly observers—they look and listen, allowing the patients as much control and being as unintrusive as possible so that the patients are free to behave in their most characteristic way.
5. During the contract situations, professionals go from the observer's role to that of negotiators. They still have to be able to listen to what clients want but now they can be more intrusive, pointing out the reality factors involved. Therapists usually know already what they would like to offer so the job at this point is to sell as much of the package as they can to the patient. As a result, at times it helps to be engaging and even a little flattering. It also helps to be enthusiastic about the proposed treatment.
6. The behaviors that are useful during the treatment situation are impossible to generalize. They vary according to the personality style of the patient (see Section V.A) and the specific problems and treatment goals (Sections IV.A and IV.B).

IV.E: HANDLING DIFFICULT SITUATIONS

In our work with emotionally disturbed individuals, we often have to face difficult situations. The goal of the professional is to respond to those situations in a way that is a) effective in handling the problem and b) therapeutic— designed to lower the amount of psychopathology of the patient. Below are situations that are often found troublesome. Some tips on handling them are also given. It should be obvious that when the therapist becomes more sophisticated, s/he may wish to respond in a different manner after taking into account the patient's personality style and psychopathology.

1. Personal Questions: Personal questions that involve the therapist's training or professional position may be handled as questions about treatment (see below). Two issues have to be considered in handling other personal questions:

a) Whether or not the therapist should give the information requested.

b) Whether or not the therapist should explore with the patient the reason for asking the question.

To decide on whether or not the information requested should be given, the therapist should have some idea regarding the patient's goal. Some personal questions are asked by individuals who feel nervous and vulnerable in the therapeutic relationship. Knowing something about the therapist may make the patient more at ease and increase support. Other times personal questions are asked as a way of gaining attention or control. In these cases the therapist has to evaluate whether allowing the maneuver is in keeping with the treatment plans. Personal questions asked in the spirit of being intrusive, bizarre or obnoxious should not be answered. The same applies to requests for information that will be used by the patient in a pathological way. Knowing the person's personality style helps to determine why the patient is asking. Needless to say, sometimes the therapist will miss the real goal of the patient and respond in a way that proves to be antitherapeutic. This should be seen as a situation where something was learned about the patient rather than as a "big mistake."

When the therapist decides that the answer should not be given, s/he basically responds by guiding the patient in another direction. This can be done by:

a) Introducing another issue (e.g., "You look better today, how are you feeling?")
b) Exploring the patient's motivation for asking the question (only if appropriate, see below)
c) Talking about the goals to be accomplished during the session (e.g., "The purpose of our talking together is to see how your problems can be helped. Let's not waste time on other issues.")
d) Talking about the therapist's reactions to the question (e.g., "You know, I am feeling uncomfortable. I don't want to make you feel bad, but I really don't want to answer that kind of question.")

Finally, the therapist should decide whether or not to explore with the patient the reasons for asking. This issue should be decided on the basis of the treatment plan and independently of the first issue discussed.

2. *Questions about the Treatment*: Questions about the treatment should be answered in the most truthful and objective fashion possible. The author advocates this position feeling that these questions

involve the "rights of the consumer" and that a therapist's belief that the information would not help the patient cannot negate his or her human rights.

3. *Questions about Another Patient*: Questions about another patient should not be answered because they involve the right to privacy of the other patient. Of the possible ways of avoiding the answer, the author prefers to explain truthfully to the patient that he cannot talk about another patient without his or her consent.

4. *Negative Material about Another Professional*: Occasionally a therapist faces a situation where a patient is bringing up negative material about another professional. Usually the best response is to listen and accept the patient's feelings as such, without being defensive but without agreeing in any way. The therapist should avoid siding with the patient against the other professional, most particularly if the other person is a member of the center's staff.

5. *Sexual Advances*: With sexual advances made by the patient, the therapist's job is to reject the idea without rejecting the patient or jeopardizing the therapeutic relationship. One technique that the author has found useful is to discuss the role of a therapist. This discussion usually provides a good reason for the therapist's disinterest without humiliating the patient.

6. *Hostility*: Professionals working with severely disturbed individuals commonly have to deal with a patient who is hostile. This type of problem usually starts with the patient being verbally abusive. A physical attack can be often prevented with the following moves:

a) Keep extremely calm at all times. Pay attention to your own feelings and try to remain as relaxed as possible. Speak with a soft and gentle voice when addressing the patient.
b) Have someone call for help if this is not already available (other professionals, guards or police).
c) Try to isolate the patient. This can be done by asking the patient to come to an office to discuss the problem or asking all nonprofessionals in the area to move away. (This move keeps arousing stimili from reaching the patient and protects others.)

d) Listen to the patient, allowing him or her to vent anger in a verbal manner. Try not to interrupt and never confront.

If limits have to be set, follow the recommendations below:

a) Get as much help as possible. (This "show of force" often prevents having to take physical action.)
b) Tell the patient what the limits are in a calm and gentle voice but with assurance and firmness (e.g., "Mr. Smith, I understand that you are upset and I am here to help. However, we cannot allow physical violence. Try to control yourself so that we don't have to place you in restraints.") Do not tell the patient that you are going to do something that you cannot do.
c) Do not attempt physical restraints without enough help to do the job safely, unless the patient is going to seriously harm him or herself or others at that moment.
d) If physical restraints are necessary and enough help is available, form a circle around the patient. Those at the patient's back should start the restraining process by holding his or her arms. At that point, those in front should hold the feet and everyone should pull, lifting the patient off the floor.
e) Use the minimal amount of force necessary to restrain the patient.

7. *Suicide Calls or Threats*: The method prescribed for handling suicidal calls or threatening calls is to be warm and friendly and to encourage the patient to continue talking. An attempt should be made to evaluate the risk involved (see Section VI.B) and to obtain an address from the caller. If the risk is eminent, the police or fire department should be called. An effort should be made, however, to obtain the patient's permission to call for help and establish a contract with the patient that s/he will not do anything before help arrives.

8. *Therapist's Strong Feelings*: A patient may sometimes evoke strong feelings in the therapist. Sometimes these feelings are the type that would be felt by any therapist handling the patient (an insulting or overcontrolling patient may tend to evoke anger or fear, an anxious patient tends to make the therapist anxious, a sexy patient may be found sexually arousing, etc.) At other times, these feelings may be the therapist's own personal reaction to the patient due to

personal past experiences (countertransference). Although sometimes acting on the therapist's feelings may be therapeutic, most often it is not. Appropriate handling requires a) awareness of the personal feelings and b) the ability to behave in a therapeutic manner in spite of the personal feelings. These situations are probably the most difficult, but perhaps they are also the situations that differentiate the outstanding therapist from the rest.

V Treatment Methods

V.A: FUNDAMENTALS OF INDIVIDUAL THERAPY

1. Individual therapy usually has one or more of the following goals:
   a) To give the patient a *supportive* relationship so that, feeling less threatened, the patient is able to function at a higher level or to continue functioning at the present level without deterioration.
   b) To increase the level of *understanding* that the patient has about him or herself or environment.
   c) To establish a relationship that allows the patient to *work through* a childhood conflict.
   d) To help the patient *change* him or herself or the environment so that life becomes less stressful.
2. It should be noted that any of the goals above are appropriate for individual therapy, singly or in combination with another. However, they should be in keeping with the overall treatment plan as discussed in Chapter XIX.
3. The supportive relationship is probably the most common goal of individual therapy. The reasons for this are that:
   a) The patient may lack the ability or resources that would be necessary to support the other goals (see Section IV.B for further discussion).
   b) Perhaps with the exception of the Antisocial Personality and the Substance Abuse Disorders, it is often felt that the supportive relationship is a necessary condition for pursuing the other possible goals.

   The supportive relationship is a relationship which attempts to make the patient feel as comfortable and appreciated as possible. This goal can be pursued through therapeutic behaviors that are general and applicable to all patients, as well as therapeutic behaviors that are designed specifically for the particular patient. Section IV.D discussed therapeutic behaviors that are applicable to all patients. Behaviors that encourage the formation of a supportive relationship in a specific patient have to take into account the individual's attitudes, interests and goals. Knowing the individual's personality style is also of great help in deciding what kind of behaviors will be seen by the patient as supportive. Table 14 gives guidelines for supportive treatment of the different personality styles. Since this type of supportive treatment goes along with the basic personality style, the therapist should also be concerned with two factors while delivering treatment:

a) That the therapist delivers only as much support as is needed and no more since delivering more would be perhaps promoting further exaggeration of the personality style. For example, in treating a patient with a dependent personality style, a therapist may want to support the patient by playing a dominant role. The therapist may authoritatively offer advice, telling the patient what to do in situations where the patient feels lost or indecisive. If the therapist were to act in the same manner in situations where the patient is able to make up his or her own mind, s/he would be actually encouraging an exaggeration of the personality style which may be encouraging pathology in the patient (a regression).
b) That the therapist does not inappropriately go along with the individual's personality bends, or foster behaviors that will get the individual into trouble.

4. To increase the level of understanding that the patient has about him or herself and the environment, the therapist has to encourage the patient to explore this area and to help the patient gain psychological insight. This is done in different ways by the different schools of therapy. However, a discussion of the different styles is beyond the scope of the present work.
5. Once a patient has an understanding of how friction is created between him or herself and the environment, the changes that are necessary in order to reduce the friction should be obvious. Often these changes follow the increased understanding without any difficulty. When the changes do not follow, one of the following factors is probably present:

TABLE 14: Characteristics of Therapeutic Interventions Thought to be Supportive to Different Personality Styles

Personality Style	*Guidelines for Supportive Therapeutic Relationships*
Schizoid	Accept the patient's inability and disinterest in interpersonal relationships. Allow him to be superficial and somewhat distant and aloof. Be ready to take a more active role in keeping the discussion going but also be comfortable with silences or discussions that are somewhat extraneous to treatment.
Avoidant	Make an effort to reassure the patient that she will not be rejected and be sure to have a positive regard for her. Be sensitive to the strength of relationship that the patient is comfortable with and do not attempt to get closer. Be aware of your own anxiety and try to be as relaxed as possible during the sessions. Try not to cancel appointments or give other indications of lack of interest.
Dependent	Play a dominant role—be willing to tell the patient what to do and to give him some assurance that he will be taken care of.
Histrionic	Give the patient as much opportunity as possible to be the center of attention. Accept whatever dramatics the patient has, laugh at her jokes, be sure to let her know often things that you like about her.
Narcissistic	Accept the premise that the patient is a superior human being. Treat him with respect and do not humiliate him in any way. Allow the patient, as much as possible, to control the relationship.
Antisocial	Accept the view of the world as a race. Try to look at the practical and material aspects of life. Try to emphasize the races that the patient has won rather than those she has lost.
Compulsive	Allow the patient to organize the sessions as much as possible. Discuss developments with him so that nothing comes as a surprise, and so that he can predict the future of the relationship. Be prepared, well organized and punctual for the sessions. Accept the premise that if one does the right thing, one will come out ahead.
Passive-Aggressive	You can tell the patient what the limits are but do not tell her what to do within those limits, allowing her as much leeway as possible. Try to avoid having the patient depend on you for anything that she can do herself. Be sure that the therapy contract is clear to the patient and that you live up to your agreement.

a) The change constitutes an approach-avoidance conflict: Some negative aspects will result from the change so that the patient is trying to avoid it.

b) The change involves habitual behavioral patterns that the patient finds difficult to break.

In the case of the approach-avoidance situation, the conflict can be real or imagined. If the result of change that the patient is trying to avoid is real, the patient can be helped to understand the situation clearly and to make an existential decision about it, accepting the consequences. If the conflict is imagined, the attempt should be made to determine its origins and work through the feelings involved.

In the case of habitual patterns that have to be changed, a behavioral approach is often helpful. The method involves determining what stimulus leads to the undesirable response, what other responses are appropriate and what system of reinforcements can be used to change the association.

6. It should be noted that when the goal of therapy is understanding or change, the resulting relationship is—by necessity—less supportive. When the goal is to increase understanding, the therapy may be more threatening because the person has to face some things about him or herself that are negative and that s/he has defended against in the past. When the goal is personality change, on the other hand, the therapeutic behaviors indicated are sometimes the opposite of what was recommended for supportive therapy, so that the relationship is perceived as uncomfortable by the patient.

7. When the goal of therapy is to increase the level of understanding or to produce some personality change, the issue of amount of change also has to be decided. The term *intensive psychotherapy* is used when the goal is to create substantial changes in the patient. For these changes to come about, in most cases the therapy sessions have to be quite frequent and the therapeutic relationship becomes very involved. Often the relationship is so involved that the mere vacationing of the therapist may be quite problematic for the patient to handle.

8. For further information the reader is referred to:
   Lewis, J. M. *To Be a Therapist: The Teaching and Learning.*

New York: Brunner/Mazel, Inc., 1978.

Reid, W.H. *Basic Intensive Psychotherapy*. New York: Brunner/Mazel, 1980.

V.B: FUNDAMENTALS OF GROUP THERAPY

1. There are many approaches to group therapy that are considered today to be *individual therapy in groups*. They pursue basically the same goals listed for individual therapy (see Section V.A) by allotting time to the different patients in one way or another. The differences in the goal chosen or the mode used to reach it are beyond the scope of the present work, but the student can review them in:

   Kaplan, H. I. and Sadock, B. J. *Comprehensive Group Psychotherapy*, Baltimore: Williams and Wilkins, 1971.
2. The use of individual therapy in groups can be of great value. However, the field of group therapy seems to be gradually unifying behind the *group process* model. This model has been repeatedly supported by the research as being of value (see Yalom below), and it involves a different concept of group work.
3. For users of the group process model *the goal of group therapy is to create a sense of group cohesiveness* among the group members. Once this basic goal is accepted, it becomes a guiding force that can be used to answer all the other issues that concern group therapy.
4. *Membership*: One of the jobs of a group therapist is to recruit and choose the members of the group. In doing so, s/he may use the following rules:
   a) A member should be an individual who has an emotional problem in which the experience of membership in a cohesive and accepting group may be helpful. It is easy to see, for instance, how patients with interpersonal anxiety or withdrawal or with feelings of unworthiness or with inability to trust others may be helped by this method. On the other hand, this may not be an appropriate treatment for an individual who has marital difficulties. A member should not be assigned to a group simply because there is room. It is the

responsibility of the therapist to evaluate the patient's needs and make sure that it is feasible to think of the group as a solution to at least some of his or her problems.

b) A member should be an individual who is compatible with the other group members. Although groups tend to be tolerant and accept a fair amount of diversity, the therapist should try not to choose individuals who are going to be very different from the rest in terms of intellectual abilities, interests, socioeconomic or educational class or severity of psychopathology. Other variables like sex, race, age or sexual orientation may also be important, depending on the individual. Errors in matching result in individuals who never quite become part of the group and often drop out after a short period of time.

5. *Administrative Duties*: The second task that a group therapist has is administering the group. This usually involves deciding on a time when the group can meet, setting limits of acceptable behavior for members of the group and keeping progress notes on the different members.
6. *Frequency of Intervention*: In general, the group therapist tries to have members communicate as much as possible with each other. The goal, therefore, is to minimize the therapist's interventions since they take away time in which the members could be interacting with one another. The exception to this rule would be, however, when the therapist feels that intervention will improve group cohesiveness.
7. *Types of Intervention*: The main purpose that a group therapist has in intervening in the group process would be improving group cohesiveness. Improving group cohesiveness is accomplished through interventions that:

   a) Allow the group to understand one member better.
   b) Help the members of the group relate better to one another.
   c) Help the members of the group see themselves as belonging to the group and see the group as a unit.

   Most helpful in achieving the goal of improving group cohesiveness are interventions that deal with the here and now and interventions that deal with group process. For further information on recognizing and dealing with group process, the following book is recommended:

Whitaker, D. S. and Lieberman, M. A. *Psychotherapy through the Group Process*. New York: Atherton Press, 1965.

8. *Mode of Intervention*: Whenever possible, the therapist should make a point through a group member rather than making the point by him or herself. For instance, if a member has been talking for some time about a topic that is boring to the rest of the members, the therapist should look around the room for a member who looks bored and ask what he or she is feeling at this time. If this fails, the therapist could turn to another member and ask what reactions he or she had to what the first member was saying. Some group therapists would feel that a point that cannot be brought out by involving a group member is not worth bringing out. Although there are certainly exceptions to that rule, it does not seem to be a bad rule of thumb to keep in mind.
9. *Use of Co-therapist*: Groups are often run by two therapists and this practice seems very beneficial. It is important, however, that the therapists themselves are compatible and that they run the group with the same goals in mind. Often this type of team work can only be achieved after some time during which the therapists meet outside of the group to discuss the group sessions.
10. A good book on group therapy that espouses these principles is:

Yalom, I. D. *The Theory and Practice of Group Psychotherapy*. Revised Edition. New York: Basic Books, 1975.

V.C: FUNDAMENTALS OF FAMILY THERAPY

1. Family therapy may be the treatment of choice when:
   a) The problem involved deals with the way the family members relate to one another *or* is assumed to be the result of a pathological family system.
   b) It is possible to motivate all the family members concerned to work towards changes in the family system.

2. Probably the most important issue in family therapy is how the family handles control (the decision-making process). Four options appear possible:*
   a) The *Overadequate-Underadequate* family has one member with all the controls. This member is seen as dominant and superior while others play a submissive role and accept his or her decisions. The play *A Doll's House* by Henrik Ibsen provides a good description of this type of relationship.
   b) The *United Front* family involves a system where no one makes the decisions. Members portray themselves as being in total agreement and reaching decisions in common, but usually do not feel that they can express any disagreement.
   c) The *Conflictual* family relationships involve constant quarrelling between family members. The reason for this is that everyone wants to have control of the decision-making process and argues frequently on issues in an attempt to establish that control. An example of this type of relationship is seen in the play *Who's Afraid of Virginia Woolf* by Edward Albee.
   d) The *Shared Control* family has different members controlling different aspects at different times.
3. The different family systems are made up of individuals with particular personality styles. Often their personality styles fit well into the system. For instance, an overadequate-underadequate system may be made up of a narcissistic husband and a dependent wife (see Section I.C); in a conflictual family there may be a histrionic and a passive-aggressive member.
4. There is a tendency among professionals to look at one of the control systems as being superior to the rest (the shared control family). Although research has supported this contention, the author has seen families that worked reasonably well and that functioned under one of the other systems. He feels that it is preferable to think of each system as having some advantages and some disadvantages. The overadequate-underadequate system, for instance, may be more effective than the rest at times of crisis. During a crisis the shared control system may not be

*Kramer, C. H., Liebowitz, B., Phillips, R. L., Schmidt, S. and Gibson, J. *Beginning Phase of Family Treatment*. Chicago: Publications of the Chicago Family Institute, 1968.

efficient enough and could easily lapse into a conflictual system. The view supported here, therefore, will be that the type of system used is not in itself a problem. Rather, family pathology would be defined as ineffective family functioning, regardless of the system used.

5. Family difficulties may be related to a specific issue or may arise out of friction within the system. Difficulties that are issue-related are differences of opinion that the family has not worked through but that do not carry any implications with regards to control. In a system that is functioning effectively, these issues do not become pathological if the family is given the opportunity to work them out.
6. Family pathology usually arises out of difficulties within the system. These difficulties may be of two types:
   a) Discomfort of one or more family members as a result of being forced to play a role in the system that does not agree with their present personality style. An example may be an overadequate-underadequate system in which an underadequate person has become, through holding a job outside the family, less submissive.
   b) Pathological behavior of one or more members who have developed the pathology as a way of fitting into the system. An example is the child in a conflictual family who started flunking school when her mother kept telling her father that his excessive drinking was affecting the children.
7. In order to do family therapy effectively, a good evaluation first has to be made of all members who are judged to be important to the family system. At the end of this evaluation, the therapist should have a clear idea of what system the family uses and what personality styles the different members have.
8. Once the evaluation is finished, the therapist has to develop a plan of action. In the case of the discomfort of a member who is forced to play a role he or she does not want to play, the family treatment plan may be to:
   a) Help the family member experiencing the discomfort to be more at ease with this role in the family.
   b) Help the system to change so that the person is no longer forced to play a distasteful role.

In the case of pathological behavior that a family member develops as a way of fitting into the system, the family treatment plan would be to:

a) Help the family member find a nonpathological way of fitting into the system.
b) Change the family system so that it does not encourage the pathological behavior.

9. The family treatment plan is put into effect by involving the whole family. Real changes are usually accomplished only when the family arrives at their own idea of what needs to be changed and their own way to change it. The job of the therapist is to guide the family in their work rather than to do any work for them. This task is easily done in the case of discomfort with a role: The therapist should encourage raising the issue of the discomfort until the family faces the problem. Then the therapist can guide them in their effort to find solutions. In the case of pathological behaviors that result from the system, the task is often harder to accomplish. However, the method should be similar—encourage the family to talk about themselves until the problem is clear; then help the family to find solutions.
10. A good reference is:

    Ferber, A., Mendelsohn, M. and Napier, A. *The Book of Family Therapy*. New York: Science House, 1972.

V.D: SPECIFIC THERAPEUTIC TECHNIQUES

The specific therapeutic techniques that follow come from many different schools of therapy. In some instances they were proposed as one among many possible techniques by the originators. In other cases, the given technique was used as the only therapeutic procedure. The author recommends a problem-oriented view in which a particular technique is carefully selected to accomplish a given goal in the patient's treatment.

It should be noted that some of these techniques also have a diagnostic use. The descriptions below, however, will address only the therapeutic value of the procedures.

1. Assertiveness Training

This technique was designed to increase assertiveness in individuals who appear to be unduly submissive. The main ideas are to

a) make clients aware of their rights
b) encourage clients to stand up for their rights
c) rehearse ways in which clients can stand up for their rights without being unduly abrasive.

For further information see Cotler, S. B. and Guerra, J. J. *Assertion Training*. Champaign, IL: Research Press, 1976.

2. Aversive Conditioning

This technique is based on the idea that if undesired behaviors are associated with repulsive or aversive stimuli, the client will lose attraction for that behavior. Prevalent examples are the induction of vomiting in alcoholics right after ingestion of alcohol, having the smoker smoke only in a repulsive or aversive place, etc. Imagery has also been used productively in developing aversive associations.

3. Behavioral Assignments

This technique is used when

a) The therapist feels that it is constructive for the client to be working on some issue before the next session.
b) The next logical step in a therapeutic progress with regard to some problem is something that should be done outside of the therapy sessions.

Examples may be having the client make a list of all the advantages and disadvantages of making a decision about which the client is conflicted, having an isolated and withdrawn client take a small step towards less isolation or withdrawal, etc.

4. Bibliotherapy

Patients who are intellectually oriented may be asked to read some literature that will enhance their cognitive understanding of the problem. Almost any professional book may be used for this purpose as long as it is related to the patient's problem. A book on general understanding of psychodynamics may also be appropriate. Be sure to allow some time for discussion of the reading material since sometimes clients misinterpret what they read in ways that may be antitherapeutic.

5. Confrontation

This technique is mainly useful when symptoms are being denied or minimized. Denial is particularly likely to be used by people with a Substance Abuse Disorder, individuals with a narcissistic personality style or a Sociopathic or Borderline Character Disorder. In the treatment of these individuals, therefore, confrontation is often an important part of that therapy. By means of confrontation, the client can be guided to face his or her resistance so that the therapeutic process can continue. It is important to keep in mind that this procedure only works as long as the therapist is perceived as remaining on the same side of the fence as the client. The author usually achieves this by:

(a) Avoiding a confrontation until a good relationship is established with the client (the timing of the confrontation can be important).
(b) Reminding the client that the confrontation is only undertaken in the interest of helping with his or her problems.

A client who perceives the therapist as an adversary will use all of his or her energy to fight the therapist, and the goal of the confrontation will not be achieved.

6. Desensitization

This technique was devised for clients who have phobic fears or apprehensions. Classical conditioning provides its theoretical basis. More specifically, desensitization attempts to associate thoughts of the feared stimulus with a relaxed mood. First, a hierarchy is constructed with situations that constitute increasing degrees of fear. For example, for a client who fears elevators, level 100 may be being in a closed elevator, level 75 may be coming into a building knowing that an elevator will have to be taken, level 50 may be standing in a small room but out of which one can leave, level 25 perhaps would be planning to do an errand on the following day in a building that has elevators, etc. The client is then helped to relax using techniques described at #15 below. Once relaxed, the client is asked to imagine vividly a situation that arouses a low level of anxiety. The moment the client feels apprehensive, he or she is to signal the therapist, to stop imagining the scene, and to get into a relaxed mood once more. This procedure is repeated until no anxiety is felt. At that point, the imagery is changed to the next situation in the previously constructed hierarchy. For further information see Wolpe, J. *Psychotherapy by Reciprocal Inhibition*. California: Stanford University Press, 1958.

7. Empty Chair Technique

The empty chair is a Gestalt strategy designed to have the client express and experience feelings toward an absent individual as vividly as possible. The client is strongly encouraged to imagine that the absent person is sitting on a chair, and is then encouraged to talk to that person and express all of his or her feelings. Descriptions of the technique can be found in Perls, F. S. *Gestalt Therapy Verbatim*. Moab, UT: Real People Press, 1969.

8. Group Exercises

The repertoire of group games or exercises is too extensive to describe in the present work. The purpose of the exercises should be to promote insight or expression of feelings among group members. They are especially helpful since the feelings evoked are often towards another member of the group, so they can be worked through rather well within the group context. The author tends to use the group exercises only when the group is not being productive. It should be noted that most of the benefit of the exercises is derived from the discussion that follows the exercises so that time should be allowed for the discussion. A good book in this area is Morris, K. and Cinnamon, M. *A Handbook of Non-verbal Group Exercises*. Springfield, IL: Charles C. Thomas, 1975.

9. Hypnosis

This procedure involves working with clients in ways that make them increasingly more susceptible to suggestions. Once they are felt to be ready, therapeutic suggestions for change are made. Prevalent uses of hypnosis are:

a) to decrease the subjective experience of pain,
b) to decrease or extinguish a particular symptom, and
c) to help clients break a habit such as smoking.

The specifics in the use of this technique are somewhat involved and are beyond the scope of the present work. The reader is referred to Erickson, M. H., Rossi, E. and Rossi, S. *Hypnotic Realities*, New York: Irvington Publishers, 1976.

10. Interpretations

This technique is used to make the client aware of a link between a previous experience and a present assumption, feeling or behavior. It is well known that the timing of the interpretations is very important. For an interpretation to be successful the client has to:

a) Be very aware of both the previous experience and the present assumptions, feelings or behaviors in question.
b) Be in an accepting mood, in other words, at a point in which it is felt that the client can at least hear, if not accept, what the therapist is about to suggest.

Further discussion can be found in Chessick, R. D. *Technique and Practice of Intensive Psychotherapy*. New York: Jason Aronson, 1974.

11. Paradoxical Instructions

A paradoxial intention involves the prescription of the symptom with the hidden goal of extinguishing it. An example of this would be to tell a compulsive patient that instead of taking five showers a day, s/he is to rearrange his or her life so as to take ten. For the procedure to work well, it must be done with complete seriousness and sincerity. If the patient complains, the therapist should use the same arguments and fears that the client uses to support the behavior. The author recommends the use of this technique with patients who are inclined to sabotage treatment. This often includes clients with a compulsive or a passive-aggressive personality style who feel that they have to be in control, as well as clients with a lot of vested interests in holding on to their pathology. Further information can be obtained from Haley, J. *Problem-Solving Therapy*. San Francisco: Jossey-Bass, 1976.

12. Rational Disputation

Albert Ellis feels that often individuals produce the wrong behavior because they hold erroneous assumptions about the world. Rational disputations involve a rational demonstration that the assumption that the client holds is erroneous. An example may be the overly shy individual who is unable to call for a date because of fear of rejection. Ellis would argue that this individual is assuming that being rejected is a terrible event and he tries to convince the client that everyone, in fact, is rejected many times in his life. The technique is particularly recommended with clients who tend to value very highly the cognitive or rational aspect of themselves. This may be particularly true in the case of compulsive individuals. For further information see Ellis, A. and Grieger, R. *Handbook of Rational Emotive Therapy*. New York: Springer, 1977.

13. Reflexive Explorations

Reflexive explorations are statements in which the therapist rephrases what the client said. When done well, the rephrasing a) adds some meaning to what the client said and b) encourages the client to go on exploring his or her feelings. An example may be the following interaction:

C: I had a very hard time when my wife left me.

T: Yes, I can see by your expression that you still have a lot of feelings about it.

Notice that the therapist is adding his or her perception of the client's present state and leaving the comment open-ended in a way that encourages the client to continue.

This is an extremely useful technique that can be used frequently. The author feels, however, that it can also be overused: Its goal is to explore and make clients aware of their feelings. The reader should keep this in mind and not use the technique when this goal is not being pursued. Further help can be obtained from Rogers, C. R. *Client Centered Therapy*. Boston: Houghton Mifflin, 1951.

14. Reinforcement

The technique of giving positive or negative reinforcement to clients is so common that some behaviorists have claimed that other techniques are simply different contexts in which reinforcement is given. Whether or not this is the case, the importance of responding appropriately to therapeutic gains or losses cannot be overemphasized. There are occasions when a therapist would want to work out with the patient a system of reinforcements with the criteria that have to be met. This may be particularly useful with

a) very regressed patients who need a very concrete system to motivate them into any kind of activity, and
b) Sociopathic or Borderline Character Disorders that may be constantly attempting to "push the limits" of acceptable behavior.

More information about systems for schedules of reinforcement can be found in Levis, D. J. (Ed.) *Learning Approaches to Therapeutic Behavior Changes*. Chicago: Aldine Publishing Co., 1970.

15. Relaxation techniques

E. Jacobson described in his book *Anxiety and Tension Control: A Psychobiological Approach* (Philadelphia: Lippincott, 1964) a procedure for muscle relaxation. The procedure involves paying attention to the muscles in one part of the body while contracting and relaxing them. The attention is then moved to another part of the body where the process is repeated. Eventually several parts may be contracted or relaxed at the same time while the attention of the subject continues to be focused in how the muscles feel. Also involved are suggestions that the subject is feeling completely relaxed, suggestions that may have a hypnotic-like effect. For readers who want to use this technique, the author also recommends a set of audiotapes made by Arnold A. Lazarus and produced by I.D.I., 166 E. Superior St., Chicago, Ill.

16. Role-Playing

This procedure involves having clients play themselves or another person in some important interaction of their life. Goals may be:

a) To have clients put themselves in the shoes of another person and realize how that person was feeling.
b) To allow histrionic clients to have the center of attention in productive way.
c) To have clients rehearse a particular role that they will have to play in real life in the future.
d) To help withdrawn clients interact with others in a highly structured setting.

The technique can be done in a group where the other group members also participate in the acting. For further information the reader is referred to *Psychodrama for the Timid Clinician* (Leveton, 1977).

17. Self-Monitoring

This procedure consists of having clients keep careful track of some data that are considered to have therapeutic importance. Examples may be feelings of clients towards their work in the course of a week, marital arguments, drinks taken, food ingested or body weight. Self-monitoring may be done with the following purposes:

a) Have the client pay attention to the data in question.
b) Create a system by which reinforcement can be obtained both externally (e.g., from the therapist) and internally (e.g., feeling of accomplishment).
c) Producing some insight (e.g., that the client is drinking too much).

18. Transactional Analysis

This technique involves the analysis of an interpersonal pattern of behavior that clients have established for themselves. As Berne pointed out, often this pattern of behavior has its own reward so that clients get into a vicious cycle that is hard to break. In analyzing the interpersonal pattern, the therapist may hope to clarify the role that clients are playing and to have them decide what they have to do in order to break the vicious cycle. The recommended reading is Berne, E. *Games People Play*. New York: Ballantine Books, 1964.

19. Thought Control

This procedure involves teaching clients to focus their attention on some sort of imagery when distracting, obsessive or disturbing thoughts come to their minds. This method can be best used with:

a) Individuals who are disturbed by particular thoughts, as in the case of obsessive patients.

b) The management of patients with chronic pain.

V.E: FUNDAMENTALS OF DRUG TREATMENT

1. The importance of therapeutic drugs in the treatment of emotional disorders cannot be denied. As a result, psychologists find themselves frequently dealing with individuals who take psychotropic medications or having to evaluate individuals for possible medication referrals.
2. Some familiarity with the available drugs and their effects is of great value in making these assessments. Tables 15-20 present a summary of the drugs available and their specifications.
3. The contraindications for a particular drug appearing in the tables are subject to medical evaluation and are not always sufficient reason for not using the drug. Whenever the psychologist knows that one of these contraindications is present, however, this information should be given to the consulting psychiatrist.
4. Most of the possible side effects are seldom seen. An exception to this rule, however, are the *extrapyramidal* symptoms frequently seen with the use of major tranquilizers or tricyclic antidepressants. These side effects may be suppressed with the use of antiparkinsonian agents. The extrapyramidal symptoms may include:

   a) Akathisia or restlessness with inability to sleep, a compulsion to walk and an inability to be still.

TABLE 15: Hypnotic Sedatives

Other Name: "Sleepers"
Actions:
1. Alleviation of anxiety
2. Sedation, induction of sleep (for brief or intermittent use)

Side Effects:
1. Dizziness, drowsiness, confusion
2. Upset stomach, nausea, vomiting
3. Headache "hangover"
4. Addictive unless otherwise specified

Contraindications: Hazardous occupation that requires alertness
Delay: Varies, see below

Drug Type	*Trade Name*	*Generic Name*	*Specific Actions*	*Dosage (mg)*
Barbiturates	Seconal	Secobarbital	Quick action	100-200
	Amytal	Amobarbital		100-200
	Tuinal	(combination of above)		50-200
	Nembutal	Pentobarbital	Quick action	100-200
	Luminal	Phenobarbital	Long acting	100-320
Nonbarbiturates	Noctec	Chloral-Hydrate	Quick action	250-1000
	Felsules		Nonaddictive	
	Kessodrate			
	Dalmane	Flurazepam	Quick action	15-60
	Doriden	Glutethimide	Very addictive	250-500
	Noludar	Methyprylon		50-300
	Placidyl	Ethchlorvynol		100-750
	Quaalude	Methaqualone	Very addictive	150-300

b) Dyskinesias and dystonias which may include jerking or spastic movements, upward deviation of the eyes, spasms of the neck and in severe cases, spasms of the mouth and pharynx with inability to speak or swallow.

c) Parkinsonian Syndrome or Parkinsonism which includes tremors, muscular rigidity of limbs and face (mask-like facies) and slowness or scarcity of movements, with lack of associated movements such as arm swing.

5. The extrapyramidal effects tend to disappear after a period of time. As a result, the usual technique is to add the antiparkinsonian drug when the symptoms appear and plan to reduce and discontinue this medication four months thereafter. At that point

TABLE 16: Minor Tranquilizers

Other Names: Antianxiety Agents

Actions:
1. Reduction of anxieties or tensions for periods of acute stress
2. Decrease of motor activity
3. Relaxation of muscles
4. Detoxification of alcohol or drug addicted patients

Side Effects:
1. Lethargy, drowsiness, dizziness or disorientation
2. Lack of coordination
3. Skin rashes
4. Increased sensitivity to alcohol
5. Tendency towards habit formation
6. Menstrual irregularities
7. Jaundice
8. Bone marrow suppression

Contraindications:
1. Pregnancy
2. Children under six
3. Hazardous occupation that requires alertness

Delay: One hour

Drug Type	*Trade Name*	*Generic Name*	*Specific Actions*	*Dosage (mg.*
Benzodiazepines	Librium	Chlordiazep-oxide	Safer in case of OD	15-300
	Valium	Diazepam		5-60
	Serax	Oxazepam		30-120
Carbamates	Equanil	Meprobamate	Unsafe and addictive	400-1600
	Miltown	"		
Diphenylmethane	Atarax	Hydroxyzine		75-400
	Vistaril	"		"

the symptoms may not reappear, even when the individual continues to take the psychotropic drug. This procedure encourages discontinuing medications that the patient no longer needs.

6. About 5% of the patients who take antipsychotic medications for some period of time develop *tardive dyskinesia*. This syndrome is characterized by a sucking-like puckering of the lips; chewing, licking or pursing movements of the tongue or mouth; or choreiform movements of the extremities. Tardive dyskinesia is irreversible in most cases and there is no known treatment. If detected, the drug should be discontinued if at all possible. If the risk of relapse is too great, Mellaril, which is the least

TABLE 17: Major Tranquilizers

Other Names: Antipsychotics, Neuroleptics

Actions:
1. Orders the thought process
2. Decreases motor activity
3. Reduces delusions and hallucinations
4. Reduces tensions and anxieties

Side Effects:
1. Extrapyramidal symptoms (see text for description)
2. Lack of coordination, difficulty and pain in movement
3. Tardive dyskinesia (see text)
4. Dizziness, drowsiness, weakness, confusion or stupor
5. Dryness of mouth and throat
6. Nasal congestion
7. Nausea, vomiting, constipation or diarrhea
8. Urinary disturbance
9. Blurred vision
10. Drop of blood pressure when standing up, tachycardia
11. Inhibition of ejaculation (especially Mellaril)
12. Menstrual irregularities
13. Skin oversensitivity to sun, skin rashes
14. Lowering of seizure threshold, convulsions
15. Jaundice
16. Weight gain

Contraindications:
1. Previous sensitivity
2. Comatose states, brain damage
3. Previous intake of large amounts of alcohol, barbiturates or narcotics
4. Hazardous occupation that requires alertness

Delay: Several days

Drug Type		*Trade Name*	*Generic Name*	*Specific Actions*	*Dosage (mg.)*
Phenothiazines	Aliphatic	Thorazine	Chlorpromazine	Strong sedative effect	50-1000
Phenothiazines	Piperazine	Stelazine Trilafon Prolixin Repoise Compazine	Trifluoperazine Perphenazine Fluphenazine Butaperazine Prochlorperazine	1. Low sedative effect 2. Prolixin Decanoate is long-acting, injectable form 3. Prone to side effect #1	5-30 12-64 1-20 15-100 10-40
Phenothiazines	Piperidine	Quide Serentil Mellaril	Piperacetazine Mesoridazine Thioridazine	Not prone to side effect #1, 3	10-160 50-400 50-800
Butyrophenones		Haldol	Haloperidol	1. Prone to side effect #1 2. Low sedative effect	2-100
Thioxanthenes		Taractan Navane	Chlorprothixene Thiothixene		25-600 5-30
Indolone		Moban	Molindone	Low sedative effect	25-400
Dibenzoxazepine		Loxitane	Loxapine	1. Strong sedative effect 2. Marked side effect #1, 14	20-100
Phenothiazine and Tricyclic		Triavil Etrafon	Perphenazine and Amitriptyline	Combination anti-psychotic and anti-depressant	

TABLE 18: Antidepressants

Actions:
1. Mood elevation
2. Reduction of psychomotor retardation
3. Increase of motivation and optimism

Side Effects:
1. Extrapyramidal symptoms (see text for description)
2. Lack of coordination, difficulty and pain in movement
3. Dizziness, drowsiness, weakness, confusion or stupor
4. Dryness of mouth and throat
5. Nausea, vomiting, constipation or diarrhea
6. Urinary disturbance
7. Blurred vision
8. Drop in blood pressure when standing up
9. Tachycardia (rapid heart rate), palpitations, arrhythmia
10. Lowering of seizure threshold, convulsions
11. Accelerated psycho-motor activity
12. Activation of psychotic symptoms like hallucinations and delusions
13. Insomnia
14. Weight gain or loss
15. Perspiration

Contraindications:
1. Prostatic hypertrophy (with tricyclics)
2. Glaucoma (with tricyclics)
3. Recent myocardial infarction
4. Arrhythmia

Delay: Two to four weeks

Drug Type	*Trade Name*	*Generic Name*	*Specific Actions*	*Dosage (mg.)*
Tricyclics	Elavil	Amitriptyline		50-225
	Norpramine	Desipramine		75-200
	Tofranil	Imipramine		50-225
	Aventyl	Nortriptyline		20-100
	Vivactyl	Protriptyline		10-60
	Sinequan	Doxepin HCl		40-200
MAO Inhibitors	Marplan	Isocarboxazid	Excessive toxicity	10-50
	Nardil	Phenelzine	Excessive toxicity	15-75
	Parnate	Tranylcyptomine	Excessive toxicity	10-30

likely to produce this disorder, may be used after informed consent has been obtained.

7. It must be kept in mind that a number of drugs may induce psychiatric reactions or complicate and aggravate previously existing conditions. The therapist should consult the reference

TABLE 19: Lithium Carbonate

Actions: Treatment of Manic Depressive Illness
1. Decrease of elation and acceleration of psychomotor activity to manic states
2. Increase of optimism, motivation and psychomotor activity in depressed states

Side Effects:
1. Nausea, vomiting, diarrhea or abdominal pain
2. Muscular weakness
3. Sluggish or dazed feeling
4. Thirst and excessive urination
5. Fine hand tremor

Intoxication produces drowsiness, tremors, slurred speech, convulsions and coma

Contraindications:
1. Thyroid deficiency
2. Renal deficiency
3. Liver deficiency
4. Cardiovascular disease
5. Patients on Diuretics

Delay: One to three weeks

Trade Name	*Generic Name*	*Specifications*	*Dosage (mg.)*
Lithonate Liphane Lithotabs Eskalith	Lithium Carbonate	Must reach blood levels of 0.8 to 1.2 milliequivalents per liter for therapeutic effect. Toxic above 2.0 mEq/li	300-2500

book given below or a physician whenever there is any questions about a medication that the patient is taking.

8. Consulting a psychiatrist appropriately is a bit of an art. For the psychologist this involves:
   a) Passing along the information that the psychiatrist will need. This information may include a psychiatric and medication history, present and past medical illnesses of importance, the present mental status, psychotropic medications used by the patient and his or her blood relatives and their response to them.
   b) Approaching the situation as one professional consulting another. On the one hand, the psychologist is not asking for

TABLE 20: Antiparkinsonians

Actions: Supression of Extrapyramidal Side Effects (see text)
Side Effects: 1. Low blood pressure or tachycardia (fast heart rate)
2. Dry mouth, nervousness or blurred vision
3. Weakness and inability to move some muscles
4. Mental confusion or excitement
Contraindications: 1. Children under three
2. Glaucoma
Delay: Ten to 20 minutes when injected

Drug Type	*Trade Name*	*Generic Name*	*Specific Actions*	*Dosage (mg.)*
Anticholinergic	Cogentin	Benztropine		0.5-6
	Artane	Trihexyphenidyl		2-15
Antihistaminic	Benadryl	Diphenhydra-mine		50-200
Other	Symmetrel	Amantadine	Reduced Side Effects	50-300

a personal favor. On the other hand, the psychiatrist is not a prescription-writing machine; s/he is a highly trained professional who has much to contribute to the treatment of the patient.

c) Having realistic expectations. In order to be legally safe and to insure that the right medication and dosage are used, the physician has to have a certain amount of contact with the patient. Psychiatrists differ in the amount of contact that they feel is needed, so this has to be worked out. The patient and the psychologist also have to be comfortable with the amount of involvement that the psychiatrist intends to have.

d) Making an effort to find one or more psychiatrists with whom the psychologist feels comfortable collaborating. The situation where one of the professionals involved has a strong dislike for the other or does not see the other as competent is not conducive to a good collaborative treatment plan. Needless to say, a great effort has to be made so that any problems in the relationship between the two professionals do not end up jeopardizing the treatment of the patient.

9. The following abbreviations are often used in connection with medications:

   pc = after meals
   hs = at bedtime
   qd = once a day
   qh = once an hour
   bid = twice a day
   tid = three times a day
   qid = four times a day
   prn = when needed. This abbreviation is often followed by some instructions to be used in determining when the medication is needed. For example: Dalmane, 15mg, hs, prn for inability to sleep.
   stat = to be given immediately
   po = by mouth
   im = intramuscularly (by injection into the muscle)
   iv = intravenous (injected into the vein)
   gr = gram
   mg = milligram

10. Further information about medications can be obtained from a recent edition of the *Physician's Desk Reference*, commonly called the *PDR* (Oradell, NJ: Medical Economics, Inc.) or from a recent edition of *AMA Drug Evaluations* (Chicago: American Medical Association).

VI Additional Issues

VI.A: THE CLINICAL RECORD

1. A complete clinical record includes three parts:
   a) The Data Base
   b) The Treatment Progress
   c) A Termination Note or Treatment Summary
2. The Data Base section consists of the basic information about the patient necessary before the appropriate treatment plan can be designed. The information is usually acquired through a diagnostic interview (see Section III.A) and may include:
   a) A general information section with the patient's:
      —age, sex, ethnic background and race
      —physical description
      —marital status
      —members of household
      —occupation and socioeconomic status
   b) The presenting complaint or reason why treatment is sought
   c) A mental health history (a review of previous reasons for seeking treatment, type of treatment obtained and results)
   d) A mental status evaluation (see Section III.B)
   e) An educational and occupational history
   f) A social history
   g) A medical history or "Review of Systems"*
   h) The results of a physical examination*
   i) The problem list (see Section IV.A)
   j) The treatment plan (see Section IV.B)
3. A progress note should be written occasionally (ideally every time the patient is seen) summarizing the current status of the patient's problems and treatments.
4. At the time of termination some type of closing note should be

---

*Usually only done with hospitalized patients.

written. This note may be as brief as to include only the reason for termination or may consist of a review of all the problems, the progress in treatment and their current status.

5. The Discharge Summary, usually required with hospitalized patients, is like a closing note that consists of:
   a) Presenting complaint
   b) Psychiatric history
   c) Mental status at the time of admission
   d) Physical exam results
   e) Treatment administered
   f) Changes on the mental status
   g) Discharge plans
6. The thoroughness of the record varies considerably from one setting to the other. The emphasis on good record-keeping is growing, however. This emphasis seems appropriate since a good record:
   a) Forces the therapist to collect and organize all the necessary information about the patient
   b) Provides a way for others to support or continue the work of the therapist
   c) Provides the only part of the therapist's work that can be easily scrutinized, as when the records are requested by a court of law.
7. An example of a complete clinical record is given below. Note that the record belongs to the same patient presented in the example of an interview in Section III.A.

Example of a Clinical Record

Name: Mr. P. F. *Age:* 24
Race: Black American
Address: 1224 Orwell Street, Chicago, IL
Phone: 463-1975 *Marital Status*: Single
Occupation: Unemployed Laborer

Presenting Complaint:

Mr. F. states that he was being pursued by former friends because they are into drugs and might have felt that he was an informer. He had tried getting police protection but they reportedly took what he had to say lightly. The patient stated that he started feeling this way about three months ago when he came to the Chicago area seeking employment. The patient came to the hospital in order to find a safe place and does not see himself in need of treatment. Mr. F. also stated that he went to the Bible and it was revealed to him that he should come to this hospital.

Mental Health History:

Mr. F. stated that he had never received treatment in the past. About one year ago, however, while he was in the military service, he felt that some of his supervisors wanted to get rid of him and deny him—for some unexplainable reason—a military career. He admitted having been in the hospital some time before discharge from military service but kept saying that he was only admitted because he needed a brain scan.

Mental Status:

Mr. F. was dressed very neatly and cleanly. He tended to relate in a suspicious and evasive manner, asking the examiner for trivial reassurances before the interview and wanting to know all the specifics of what was about to take place. Obsessive-compulsive traits were obvious. Intellectually, the patient appeared to be of normal abilities or slightly below. He was verbal and coherent and able to express himself. There were no indications of intellectual or memory impairments. In his evasiveness, the patient was quite circumstantial, giving all kinds of trivial details and seldom getting down to a clear answer. Some persecutory delusions were noted and perhaps even some ideas of reference concerning the Bible. Although he talked about being persecuted as a response to questioning, he did not appear to be preoccupied with these thoughts and was not fearful. His emotions were appropriate to the content of the conversation and the prevailing mood was serious but well within the normal limits. The anxiety and the activity levels were also unremarkable.

Educational and Occupational History:

Mr. F. dropped out of high school before finishing to enlist in the Air Force. He served in the military for the full four-year term although he apparently had some problems there. Upon discharge he stayed in Michigan where he had been stationed for nine months during which time he worked for one day at a department store during the Christmas holidays in his home town. Three months ago he moved to Chicago where he reportedly has been looking for work unsuccessfully.

Social History:

Mr. F. was brought up in a southern state, the oldest among three children. As a teenager he developed some severe conflict with his parents since he felt that they favored his youngest sister and were not fair to him. This conflict culminated in his enlistment as a way to get away from the home.

Once in the service he developed some friends but was better characterized as a loner. He blames the isolation on his supervisors who would give him the type of job that did not have much contact with others. Nevertheless, he was not even able to form relationships with his co-workers. Since his discharge, he has also remained fairly isolated, single, and does not date.

Medical History:

During the review of the systems, the only medical complaint was that of a recurrent headache during the past few months. He described it as being across the forehead and involving constant pain which increased when he tried to concentrate.

Physical Evaluation:

The physical examination revealed a well-nourished 24-year-old black male. Both the physical examination and the Review of the Systems were within normal limits except for the presence of a heart murmur.

Problem List:

1. Persecutory delusions, ideas of reference
2. Circumstantiality of thought
3. Suspiciousness
4. Lack of social and community resources, lack of job

5. Inability to form relationships
6. Heart murmur

Treatment Plan:

1. Persecutory Delusions
   a) Supportive treatment—allow patient to feel as comfortable as possible in ward
   b) Discourage discussion of this topic
   c) Medicate (Dr. M. has agreed to prescribe an antipsychotic drug)
2. Circumstantiality of Thought
   a) Make patient aware of problem
   b) Try to help patient respond in concise manner
   c) Follow plan under #1
3. Suspiciousness
   a) Do not ask for information that the patient is not comfortable in giving
   b) Follow recommendation under #1
4. Lack of Resources
   a) Explore possibility of patient returning to home town
   b) If patient intends to stay in area, involve social service and patient in exploring community resources
   c) Make more concrete plans in future
5. Inability to Form Relationships
   a) Be supportive
   b) Make every attempt to set up a milieu in which patient will not be rejected
   c) Assign patient to group therapy and activities and encourage patient to attend
   d) Explore possibility of involvement in long-term therapy. If possible, find suitable follow-up setting.
6. Heart Murmur
   a) Send patient to Cardiac Service for further evaluation

Progress Notes, Lab Reports, Consultation Reports, etc.

Example of a Discharge or Termination Summary

Name: P. F. *Age:* 24
Race: Black American
Address: 1224 Orwell Street, Chicago, IL
Phone: 463-1975 *Marital Status:* Single
Occupation: Unemployed laborer
Diagnosis: Paranoid Schizophrenic Disorder (295.31)

Presenting Complaint:

Mr. F. asked for hospitalization when he felt that he was being persecuted by former friends and that the hospital would provide a safe place to hide.

Mental Health History:

The patient claims to have never received treatment before, but there were indications of poor functioning prior to the present crisis.

Mental Status on Admission:

The previous description would be included here.

Physical Exam and Lab Reports:

The previous description would be included here with the abnormal laboratory findings added.

Course of Treatment:

A consultation with Dr. M. led to prescriptions of an antipsychotic medication (Haldol, 10 mg., bid) as well as an anticholinergic drug to take care of side effects (Cogentin, 1 mg., bid). Supportive individual therapy eventually led to the establishment of a trusting relationship between the therapist and the patient. As the patient began to feel more at ease in the ward, he was initiated in a therapy group intended to be supportive and was encouraged to take part in other ward activities.

After some substantial improvement had taken place, the patient's family was called. At first they were unenthusaistic to the idea of having the patient back, but their feelings changed through repeated conversations with the staff. It was possible in this way to enlist their cooperation and support.

Current Mental Status:

At the time of termination, Mr. F. was able to come to the point in his conversations without the trivial details and circumstantiality seen on admission. The persecutory delusions and religious preoccupations had vanished and all other indications of severe emotional disorder had disappeared.

Discharge Plan:

Dr. M. provided two weeks of the medications listed above for the patient. Mr. F. plans to go back to live with his parents. A referral has been made for follow-up treatment at Midway Center. The patient was given an appointment for the initial evaluation on August 30.

VI.B: DISPOSITIONAL DECISIONS

1. It is of extreme importance to be able to decide on the type of mental health setting that would best meet the client's needs. In the worst cases, dispositional mistakes may lead to the loss of human lives. In less extreme cases, the failure to match patients and settings is still costly since it leads to early dropouts and failures in therapy.
2. From a dispositional point of view, it is helpful to consider a) the *intensiveness* of treatment of the different types of facilities, and b) the amount of *restriction* that a particular type of facility places on the patient. Often these two issues are related so that the facilities delivering the most intensive treatment (e.g., hospitals) are also the most restrictive. Exceptions are psychoanalysis and psychoanalytic-oriented treatments which may be very intensive but not very restrictive.
3. For deciding on a disposition, the *rule of thumb is to use the least intensive and restrictive setting* that may fulfill the client's needs. This rule seems appropriate for several reasons. First, it represents a good allocation of professional resources since the more ex-

pensive, intensive treatment is only used when extremely necessary. Second, it avoids giving clients the message that they are sicker than they really are. Finally, it avoids the danger of "institutionalization," having patients regress in an environment where all needs are provided for, the patients lose contact with their community and become more uncomfortable with the stresses of daily routines, etc. The prevalent exception to the rule of thumb is, again, the psychoanalytic-oriented methods which may choose to use a fairly intensive treatment with the goal of restructuring the personality make-up of clients who are not very disturbed.

4. Section VI.D discusses the different types of mental health facilities. Acquaintance with that material usually allows the practitioner to choose the least restrictive setting.
5. The present dispositional emphasis is usually to try to avoid hospitalization since that is probably the most restrictive alternative presently available. There are many times, however, when hospitalization is needed. Good examples of such instances are:
   a) When the patient may be harmful to him or herself or others (see below for further information).
   b) When the patient cannot be handled appropriately outside of the hospital due to:
      —intoxication or drug reactions
      —extreme behavioral unpredictability
      —loss of contact with reality that significantly impairs the ability to function as in the case of some, but not all, of the hallucinatory or delusional patients
      —extreme behavior as with a person who is extremely agitated, manic, bizarre or hostile.
   c) When a person needs an intensive diagnostic workup that may be better done as an inpatient.
   d) When a client needs a type of treatment that can only be done safely in the hospital. This issue applies mainly to electroshock treatment but may be also present with the administration of psychotropic drugs to an individual who presents some particular medical problems.
   e) When hospitalization makes sense in terms of a family crisis. (At times, a family may need a "vacation" from the patient,

or a family is showing extreme pathology and having the patient out of the home can help them solve their conflicts, etc.)

6. The determination of suicidal risk is difficult and has, as a result, received some attention from professionals. Tuckman and Youngman*, for instance, have developed a rating system by taking into account the risk factors. The system works by scoring one point each time that any of the following factors are present:
   a) older than 45 years
   b) male
   c) white
   d) separated, divorced or widowed
   e) lives alone
   f) unemployed or retired
   g) poor physical health in past six months
   h) mood disorder, alcoholism or another mental disorder
   i) medical care in the last six months
   j) firearms, jumping or drowning used in previous attempt
   k) attempt made during warm months
   l) attempt made during daylight hours
   m) attempt made at own or other's home
   n) person reported attempt almost immediately
   o) denies intent to kill self
   p) suicide note
   q) previous attempts.

   The scores are then interpreted as follows:

   0-5 —Low risk (suicide rate = 6.98/1000)
   6-9 —Medium risk (suicide rate = 19.61/1000)
   10-12—High risk (suicide rate = 60.61/1000)

7. In order to decide on the potential that a particular patient has for harming others, the professional should take into account
   a) The amount of anger that the individual shows when talking about it
   b) How preoccupied the individual is with the issue
   c) Whether or not the patient is actually threatening to do something

---

*Tuckman, J. and Youngman, W. F. A scale for assessing suicide risk of attempted suicides. *Journal of Clinical Psychology*, 1968, 24, 17-19.

d) Whether or not the patient has a plan of action
e) Previous history of aggressive acts
f) Previous history of impulsive, emotional acts.

8. It should be noted that if the client is judged to be potentially harmful to him or herself or to others, the professional is morally and legally required to do whatever has to be done in order to assure that everyone involved is safe. For more information about commitment procedures and other legal requirements, see Section VI.E.

VI.C THE REFERRAL PROCESS

The referral process involves matching clients with mental health facilities. Even when social workers—who have traditionally been responsible for this part of the treatment—are able to help the client with this task, making appropriate dispositions often requires that the primary therapist be acquainted with the process. What follows are the steps involved in helping a client through this process.

1. Get acquainted with the different types of mental health settings (Section VI.E) as well as with the specific facilities available in the area.
2. Choose the facility that seems to fit best the patient's needs. Make it a cooperative venture which is shared with the patient. In case of doubt, choose the least restrictive facility.
3. Be sure that the client is comfortable with the choice. If s/he is not, explore the reasons why. Then, either discuss the problems until the client is more comfortable with the decision or consider changing the decision.
4. Be sure that some member of the staff has enough contact with the facility. Be sure that they have all the information that they need. Avoid having the staff of this facility feel like you are dumping a patient on them. Try to make them feel that the referral is made only on the basis of the patient's needs.
5. Encourage both the patient and the facility to inform you of any difficulties. When difficulties arise, they should be seen as part of a process through which the patient's needs are discovered.
6. A patient's rejection or return is usually due to one or more of the following:

   a) The setting to which the patient was referred does not fulfill his or her needs
   b) The patient had trouble establishing him or herself at the center
   c) The patient is "acting out"
7. If the setting was inappropriate, another center should be chosen and the process should be repeated.
8. If the client had trouble establishing him or herself, this issue should be addressed in a manner that includes the staff of the new center.
9. Finally, if the client is acting out, the issue has to be explored and understood. Acting out usually is due to the client's dislike for some aspect of the referral. Understanding the dynamic issues involved helps the therapist to decide on what course of action to take. It is often appropriate to point out to the client that acting out usually leads to more restrictive and less appropriate dispositions. A new attempt can then be made to involve the client in the decision-making process and have him or her cooperate with the disposition.

VI.D: MENTAL HEALTH SETTINGS

1. There are three kinds of mental health facilities:
   a) Treatment settings
   b) Placement settings
   c) Settings that combine treatment and placement
2. *Treatment facilities* include:
   a) Private Office Practice of psychiatrists, psychologists* or social workers. Depending on the office, any of the following may be offered:
      —assessments and evaluations
      —individual psychotherapy
      —group psychotherapy
      —family or marital therapy
      —drug therapy
      Attention should be paid to the orientation of the therapist.

---

*The *National Registry* is published annually and lists all psychologists recognized by the Registry as qualified to provide independent treatment of patients.

Unfortunately, this type of information is not presently readily available.

b) *Mental Hygiene Clinics* or *Outpatient Clinics* which may employ any one of the mental health professionals and offer any one of the treatments listed above.
c) *Alcoholic Treatment Programs* usually catering to detoxified, nonpsychotic patients who are judged to be motivated to work on their drinking problem.
d) *Drug Treatment Programs* which are similar to the alcohol treatment programs but for users of other drugs instead.
e) *Vocational Rehabilitation Programs* for the evaluation and counseling of clients who have occupational problems.
f) *Day Hospital Programs* offering structured and therapeutic activities daily for patients that need a program of this type before they can resume a normal life in the community.
g) *Sheltered Workshops* geared to patients that need to get back into the routine and responsibility of holding a job.
h) *Sustaining Care Programs* which are designed for chronic patients who need daily structure and involvement but who are expected to remain at their present level of functioning.

3. Among the *placement settings*, the following are found:
   a) Nursing Homes—housing facilities for clients who are medically sick.
   b) Retirement Homes—facilities for clients who are old but not seriously ill.
   c) Intermediate Care Facilities—these centers, also called "halfway houses," were originally meant to provide housing during a period of transition after patients were discharged from a hospital but while they were not yet able to resume independent living in the community. Although some continue to function in that manner, most intermediate care facilities also accept patients who are planning to stay there indefinitely.
4. Finally, *live-in treatment facilities*, include:
   a) Hospitals—these facilities are costly and very restrictive to the patient. As a result, they should only be used when they are clearly needed and only for the period of time in which they are needed. Good reasons for hospitalization, however, do exist as indicated in Section VI.B.

It should be noted that most hospitals presently have a very brief length of stay. (The average is usually under 30 days.) As a result, hospitalization should be seen as a measure to cope with a time of crisis. Occasionally a patient is in definite need of hospitalization for a prolonged period of time. In these cases a hospital has to be found that is willing to undertake this task.

b) Alcohol or Drug Detox Programs—these facilities give inpatient care for a period of several days for the purpose of detoxifying a patient. Often, however, they are not equipped to handle patients who present complications (e.g., toxic psychosis, severe medical problems, suicidal risk, etc.)

c) Alcohol or Drug Treatment Programs—these centers are for patients who are motivated to fight their habit when it is thought that they would not be able to do so on an outpatient basis. Commonly the programs require that the individual be detoxified before admission.

d) Vocational Rehabilitation Programs—these facilities are for clients who are in need of vocational rehabilitation and are so impaired at the present time that they cannot be helped through an outpatient program.

5. In offering the best treatment possible, it is often desirable to combine what different facilities have to offer. For instance, a patient may be seeing a private practitioner for emotional problems and going to a vocational rehabilitation program besides. Patients who are sent to intermediate care facilities are often linked to sustaining care programs if a program of that sort does not exist at the intermediate care center. Obviously many more examples could be given. The task of the professional is to set up a program that makes sense for a particular patient. Whether this can be done with a single program or with a combination is unimportant.

VI.E: LEGAL ISSUES

It is of extreme importance for professionals to have some knowledge of the law so that they can operate in a safe and responsible fashion. The material that follows reflects the law in the State of

Illinois and should be altered, where appropriate, to comply with the laws of particular states.

1. Quality of Care

Professionals are legally responsible for delivering the best care they can in the most "humane" manner and using the "least restrictive" option possible.

2. Basic Rights

At all times clients should have complete freedom to practice their religion and to communicate to whomever they please through mail, telephone or face-to-face encounters. Patients are to be allowed to possess and use personal property and live-in centers should provide adequate storage space. A facility, however, can restrict certain objects when this is necessary for the protection of their clients.

Clients have a right to be informed in the most truthful way possible about the following matters:

a) The type of treatment being offered
b) Other alternatives to the treatment that is being offered
c) Their right to refuse treatment
d) Their right to consult a lawyer, the Mental Health Advocacy Commission or anyone else

3. Restriction of Rights

When necessary in order to prevent clients from causing physical harm to themselves or to others, their rights can be restricted. This restriction usually involves restraints or seclusion of the patient and should be done according to the following rules:

a) The "least restrictive" alternative should always be used.
b) If a physician is available, a written order has to be signed by him or her.
c) In the case of an emergency when a physician is not available, any qualified person can order the restriction but this order has to be signed by a physician within the next eight hours.
d) No order of this type should be valid for more than 12 hours.

e) A person on seclusion has to be checked every 15 minutes by a staff person.
f) Once a restriction has been employed during a 24 hour period, it cannot be used again during the next two days without a written authorization by the facility director.
g) Once a restriction has been implemented, the following persons have to be informed in writing:
    (i) The client him or herself
    (ii) The facility director
    (iii) The parent in the case of a minor or the guardian in case of a person under guardianship
    (iv) The nearest relative or the person designated by the clients to receive such notice
    (v) The Mental Health Advocacy Commission if the patient so wishes

4. The Record

The therapist is required by law to keep a record of the patient's problems, treatment plan, therapy progress and cost.

5. The Right to Correct the Record

Clients, their parents if they are under 12, their guardians if they are legally incompetent, and the clients' advocates, have a right to inspect the clinical record or any information disclosed in the clients' behalf (see below under Confidentiality). If clients or their representatives disagree with some information present in the record, they have a right to have it modified if this is agreeable to the professional who wrote it. Otherwise, they have a right to include a statement in the record that explains their objection.

6. Confidentiality

Any information given to a professional by a patient or about a patient as part of the treatment process is to be completely confidential and cannot be released to anyone except:
a) When the patients, their parents if they are under 12, or their

guardians if they are legally incompetent, request information or request a release of the information. A release must contain:

(i) The patient or agency to whom the disclosure should be made

(ii) The purpose of such disclosure

(iii) The information to be disclosed

(iv) The date or period of time for which the release is valid

b) When therapists communicate information to their supervisors, consulting therapists, members of the agency's staff, persons conducting a peer review of the services provided or the therapists' attorneys when consulting in relation to clients.

c) When the court, after giving a chance to the clients or other interested parties to object, orders the professional to release a particular piece of information. (Notice that a therapist is not controlled by an ordinary subpoena which is often obtained without the clients' presence).

d) When the therapist must disclose particular pieces of information in order to prevent harm in cases involving any one of the following:

(i) An abused or neglected child

(ii) Commitment or competency hearings

(iii) Emergency medical care

e) When the police department wants to know if a particular person is emotionally disturbed in order to determine if that person is disqualified from owning a gun.

In all cases, only the particular piece of information needed should be disclosed and a note should be made in the record showing the information disclosed and to whom the disclosure was made.

7. Commitment or Incompetency

Patients who are dangerous to themselves or to others can be forced to submit to treatment after a court hearing on the matter. The procedure is as follows:

a) A petition has to be filled out by any adult who feels that the patient is in need of involuntary hospitalization. A copy if the petition has to be given to the client, guardian if any, and any two other persons if the client so wishes.

b) The patient has to be informed of his or her rights, the purpose of the examinations and the fact that any information that s/he gives may be used in court to support the need for commitment. The patient should also know that s/he has a right to legal counsel and does not have to talk at all if s/he does not want to. A copy of the petition has to be given to the client, guardian if any, and and does not have to talk at all if s/he does not want to.
c) A professional (physician, clinical psychologist, psychiatric social worker or nurse with master's degree in psychiatric nursing) has to examine the client and decide if s/he is in fact dangerous to himself or others. If the professional decides that this is the case, s/he has to fill out a certificate testifying to that effect.
d) A police officer can then be called to transport the patient to a State Mental Health Facility where the patient will wait for the court proceedings.
e) Within 24 hours the patient has to be examined by a psychiatrist who cannot be the same person that filled out the first certificate. After examining the patient, this psychiatrist fills out a second certificate, also testifying that the patient is in need of involuntary admission.
f) All documents have to be taken to the court at this time. The court has to schedule a hearing on the matter within the next five days.

The same procedure as above should be followed in the case of a person judged to be incompetent or unable to take care of him or herself or property.

8. Admissions

A client in need of inpatient treatment may be admitted to a live-in facility under any of the following contracts:

a) The Informal Admission—this type of admission is the least restrictive and should be used whenever it is appropriate. Patients using this type of admission should be informed in writing and orally of their right to be discharged upon request during working hours.
b) The Voluntary Admission—this type of admission should be used whenever it is felt that the patient may constitute a danger to him

or herself or to others but is willing to apply for admission. A written application form should be used. This type of admission allows the facility to hold the patient for five days after a request for discharge has been received. At the end of that period, if the patient is judged to be potentially harmful, the commitment procedure has to be initiated. Twenty days after admission, the director of the facility has to review the record and request from the patient an affirmation of a wish to stay. The patient's response has to be documented in the record. This procedure then has to be repeated every 60 days thereafter.

c) Administrative Admission—this admission is to be used in the case of a mentally retarded person who is not able to make the decisions involved in requesting admission. The procedure is as follows:
   (i) The application has to be filled out by the client if s/he is capable and 18 or older, by the guardian if the client is incompetent or by the parent if the client is a minor.
   (ii) The client has to be evaluated by a clinical psychologist and a physician; both of them have to write a report of their evaluation, recommend the Administrative Admission and give their reasons for this recommendation.
   (iii) The client and any interested person should be told of their right to object to the admission. If they do so, the rules to be followed are the same as those under the Voluntary Admission contract.

9. Insurance

Any person that works with patients should be covered under a professional liability insurance. This coverage can be obtained individually through the American Psychological Association. In most training centers, however, staff and students are covered under a policy that has been negotiated for the whole center.

10. Training

When the person who is delivering the service is not fully trained and qualified to deliver that service, two further issues are present.

The first issue is that of accurate representation—the client has a right to know that the person delivering the service is a trainee. Also, a student's work is only appropriate as long as s/he is adequately supervised. The center, the supervisor as well as the students are responsible for taking all necessary measures to assure the adequacy of this supervision.

References

AMA Drug Evaluations. Chicago: American Medical Association, published annually.

American Psychiatric Association. *Diagnostic and Statistical Manual*. Third Edition. (DSM-III) Washington: The American Psychiatric Association, 1979.

Beck, S. J., Beck, K., Levitt, E. and Molish, H. *Rorschach's Test*. New York: Grune and Stratton, 1961.

Berne, E. *Games People Play*. New York: Ballantine Books, 1964.

Bernstein, L., Bernstein, R., and Dana, R. *Interviewing—A Guide for Health Professionals*. New York: Appleton-Century, 1974.

Blanco, R. F. *Prescription for Children with Learning and Adjustment Problems*. Springfield, IL: Charles C. Thomas, 1972.

Buros, O. K. (Ed.) *The Eighth Mental Measurement Yearbook*. Highland Park, NJ: Gryphon Press, 1978.

Bush, W. J. and Waugh, K. W. *Diagnosing Learning Disabilities*. Columbus, OH: Charles E. Merrill, 1976.

Chessick, R. D. *Technique and Practice of Intensive Psycho-Therapy*. New York: Jason Aronson, 1974.

Coleman, J. C. *Abnormal Psychology and Modern Life*. Glenview, IL: Scott-Foresman, 1972.

Cotler, S. B. and Guerra, J. J. *Assertion Training*. Champaign, IL: Research Press, 1976.

Ellis, A. and Grieger, R. *Handbook of Rational Emotive Therapy*. New York: Springer, 1977.

Erickson, M. H., Rossi, E. and Rossi, S. *Hypnotic Realities*. New York: Irvington Publishers, 1976.

Exner, J. F. *The Rorschach Systems*. New York: Grune and Stratton, 1969.

Ferber, A., Mendelsohn, M. and Napier, A. *The Book of Family Therapy*. New York: Science House, 1972.

Froelich, R. E. and Bishop, F. M. *Clinical Interviewing Skills*. St. Louis: C. V. Mosby Co., 1977.

Freedman, A. M., Kaplan, H. I. and Sadock, B. J. (Eds.) *Comprehensive Textbook of Psychiatry*. Baltimore: Williams and Wilkins, 1975.

Gardner, E. *Fundamentals of Neurology: A Psychophysiological Approach*. Philadelphia: Saunders, 1975.

Graham, J. R. *The MMPI: A Practical Guide*. New York: Oxford University Press, 1977.

Haley, J. *Problem-Solving Therapy*. San Francisco: Jossey-Bass, 1976.

Hayes-Roth, F., Longabaugh, R. and Ryback, R. The problem-oriented medical record and psychiatry. *British Journal of Psychiatry*, 1972, 121, 27-34.

Jacobson, E. *Anxiety and Tension Control: A Psychobiological Approach*. Philadelphia: Lippincott, 1964.

Kaplan, H. I. and Sadock, B. J. (Eds.). *Comprehensive Group Psychotherapy*. Baltimore: Williams and Wilkins, 1971.

Klopfer, B., Ainsworth, M., Klopfer, W. and Holt, R. *Rorschach Technique*. New York: Harcourt Brace Jovanovich, 1954.

Kramer, C. H., Liebowitz, B., Phillips, R. L., Schmidt, S. and Gibson, J. *Beginning Phase of Family Treatment*. Chicago: Publications of the Chicago Family Institute, 1968.

Lachar, D. *The MMPI: Clinical Assessment and Automated Interpretation*. Los Angeles: Western Psychological Services, 1974.

Lazarus, A. A. *Multimodal Behavior Therapy*. New York: Springer, 1976.

Levis, D. J. (Ed.) *Learning Approaches to Therapeutic Behavior Changes*. Chicago: Aldine, 1970.

Lewis, J. M. *To be a Therapist: The Teaching and Learning*. New York: Brunner/Mazel, Inc., 1978.

Leveton, E. *Psychodrama for the Timid Clinician*. New York: Springer, 1977.

Lezak, M. D. *Neuropsychological Assessment*. New York: Oxford University Press, 1976.

Luria, A. R. *The Working Brain: An Introduction to Neuropsychology*. New York: Basic Books, 1973.

MacKinnon, R. A. and Michels, R. *The Psychiatric Interview in Clinical Practice*. Philadelphia: Saunders, 1971.

Megargee, E. I. *The California Psychological Inventory Handbook*. San Francisco: Jossey-Bass, 1972.

Millon, T. *Modern Psychopathology*. Philadelphia: Saunders, 1969.

Millon, T. and Millon, R. *Abnormal Behavior and Personality*. Philadelphia: Saunders, 1974.

Morris, K. T. and Cinnamon, K. M. *A Handbook of Non-Verbal Group Exercises*. Springfield, IL: Charles C. Thomas, 1975.

Perls, F. S. *Gestalt Therapy Verbatim*. Moab, UT: Real People Press, 1969.

Physician's Desk Reference Book. Oradell, NJ: Medical Economics, 1979.

Pruyser, P. W. *The Psychological Examination: A Guide for Clinicians*. New York: International Universities Press, 1979.

Reid, W. H. *Basic Intensive Psychotherapy*. New York: Brunner/Mazel, 1980.

Reitan, R. M. The validity of the Trail Making Test as an indicator of brain damage. *Perceptual and Motor Skills*, 1958, 8, 271-76.

Rogers, C. R. *Client Centered Therapy*. Boston: Houghton Mifflin, 1951.

Rogers, C. R. *On Becoming a Person*. Boston: Houghton Mifflin, 1967.

Sattler, J. M. *Assessment of Children's Intelligence*. Philadelphia: Saunders, 1974.

Shaw, D. J. The reliability and validity of the Halstead Category Test. *Journal of Clinical Psychology*, 1966, 22, 176-79.

Strub, R. and Black, F. *The Mental Status Examination in Neurology*. Philadelphia: F. A. Davis, 1977.

Tallent, N. *Psychological Report Writing*. Englewood Cliffs, NJ: Prentice Hall, Inc., 1976.

Tomkins, S. S. *The Thematic Apperception Test*. New York: Grune and Stratton, 1947.

Tuckman, J. and Youngman, W. F. A scale for assessing suicide risk of attempted suicides. *Journal of Clinical Psychology*, 1968, 24, 17-19.

Whitaker, D. S. and Lieberman, M. A. *Psychotherapy through the Group Process*. New York: Atherton Press, 1965.

Wolman, B. B. (Ed.). *Manual of Child Psychopathology*. New York: McGraw-Hill, 1972.

Wolpe, J. *Psychotherapy by Reciprocal Inhibition*. Stanford, CA: Stanford University Press, 1958.

Yalom, I. D. *The Theory and Practice of Group Psychotherapy*. Revised ed., New York: Basic Books, 1975.